C0-AKF-167

REFLECTIONS

REFLECTIONS

bio-psychological, psychoanalytic, philosophical, socio-political, aesthetic and personal

by

DR. ROSS THALHEIMER

PHILOSOPHICAL LIBRARY

NEW YORK

15 East 40 Street, New York, N. Y. 10016

Library of Congress Catalog Card No. 79-164910
SBN 8022-2058-4

Printed in the United States of America

TABLE OF CONTENTS

PART THREE: THE WORLD OF PHILOSOPHY

PART FOUR: ON FREUD AND THE UNCONSCIOUS

PART FIVE: ANIMISM, PSYCHOPATHOLOGY, PSYCHOTHERAPY, ETC.

PART SIX: OF THIS AND THAT

PART SEVEN: AESTHETICS AND THE ARTS

PART EIGHT: CREATIVE ANIMATION AND THE BEYOND

PREFACE

This is a volume of miscellaneous reflections, thoughts which I have wanted, for one reason or another, and with different degrees of wanting, to have a life beyond my own, even if it be a quiet life in an unread book. With regard to some of the thoughts which are being sent out from here, I confess to having the hope, if not the complete conviction, that they will be duly recognized to be of major theoretical importance. I am referring in particular, perhaps, though by no means exclusively, to what is said concerning the Basic Tendency, a nuclear idea with applications and ramifications in fields ranging from biology to philosophy and from psychology to art.

A number of other thoughts are here for which I have on the whole a less immodest level of anticipation. Some of these involve suggestions which admittedly are quite speculative and others suggestions which, though perhaps more likely to be valid, are also less unorthodox. Still other thoughts are here largely because I wanted to clarify my own thinking on a particular topic, to put down in words what I "really" believe about it. Finally there are those thoughts which seemed to come from deep inside of me rather than from my head, the quite personal and emotionally tinged thoughts which are, perhaps, more reflections *of* me than *by* me.

The book is divided into Parts and the Parts into Sections. I began its writing simply by jotting down whatever thought happened to be of special interest to me at the moment, that is, without regard to where that thought, if retained, might eventually be placed in the collection. As the collection grew, however, certain interrelationships, logical as well as substantive, began to be discernible, and hence some sort of structure. However, for better or for worse, that structure even now remains somewhat less than compelling, for though the Sections follow one another in *one* particular order, various *other* orders – I am thinking especially of the Section order in Parts VI and VIII – would no doubt be no less appropriate.

This book contains relatively few quotations from, or specific textual references to, other authors. This is in part, at least, a matter of temperamental choice. But by way of "compensation", I have included a Selected Bibliography.

Acknowledgements should be extended to so many persons, relatives and friends, teachers and colleagues, that it seems ill-fitting to single out any of them for special mention. My gratitude goes out to them all.

PART ONE

THE BASIC TENDENCY AND RELATED PRINCIPLES

THE BASIC TENDENCY

I would like to set forth a hypothesis in regard to the behavior (the responses) of living organisms. To the best of my knowledge, it is a hypothesis which has not heretofore been formulated – except, perhaps, in a manner giving it a far narrower (not to say significantly different) scope or leaving its essential concepts so loosely defined as to be all but meaningless.[1] Yet in my judgment it represents the most fundamental and richly implicative statement which can be made about organismic behavior. The hypothesis is that *there is a basic tendency in all living organisms, regardless of species, to respond in such a way as to maximize (i.e., to increase or at least to maintain) stimulation insofar as it is vitalizing and to minimize (i.e., to terminate or at least to decrease) stimulation insofar as it is devitalizing and, up to a limiting point, to do so in direct relationship to the degree to which the stimulation is, respectively, vitalizing or devitalizing.*

This basic tendency is the fundamental factor behind unlearned (or "instinctual") response patterns as it is behind learned behavior. It is revealed in the functioning of an organism as a whole and in the operation of various subordinate physiological units embraced within that whole. It is evident in the life-sustaining reactions of the simplest plants and animals and in the complicated thought processes (including the psychological defenses) of Man. (In relation to the psychological difficulties of Man, it provides a conceptual framework for a form of psychotherapy which I call "Vitalistic Psychotherapy.") It is not unlikely that we shall one day arrive at a physicochemical analysis of the tendency in terms of the attraction or repulsion of (positive and negative) electrical charges.

In subsequent Sections I shall have occasion to explore various manifestations of this Basic Tendency (hereafter usually referred to as the BT). Here let me make the following clarifying remarks in relation to my *statement* of the BT.

(1) When I speak of the "tendency" of living organisms to respond in the way specified, I am asserting that this is their characteristic or typical way of responding, that this is the way they do respond (given stimulation which is sufficiently vitalizing or devitalizing) barring organically or traumatically induced pathology.[2] Of course, organisms belonging to different species, or even different organisms falling within the same species, differ from one another in regard to the manner, the speed and the effectiveness with which they so respond. (Let me add, as a metaphysical footnote, that I do *not* conceive of this tendency as entailing the existence of any kind of extra-scientific "force" or other extra-scientific entity. What I am asserting is rather the presence of a certain *relationship* between certain *observable variables.*)

(2) By "vitalizing" stimulation is meant stimulation which serves to strengthen the life of, to increase the internal well-being of, to further the functional role of. By "devitalizing" stimulation is meant stimulation which threatens to weaken the life of, to decrease the internal well-being of, to impede the functional role of. Stated somewhat differently, we may say that *vitalizing stimulation serves to activate or to perpetuate an organism's life-sustaining processes and that devitalizing stimulation threatens to deactivate or to terminate an organism's life-sustaining processes.* Thus vitalizing stimulation may be said to be *life-serving,* devitalizing stimulation, *life-endangering.*

(3) The term "stimulation" is used in its broad biological sense to refer to excitation which, initiated either internally or externally, and either through specialized receptors or otherwise, activates a response (see numbered paragraph

9 of this Section). Various types of internal or external operants may elicit such excitation and thus serve as stimuli. Such stimuli (to use a current classification) may be mechanical, chemical, thermal, radiant or electric. (A "stimulus" is to be distinguished from a "stimulation source" and a "stimulation source" from the "internal condition" or external "stimulus object" in which that source resides. See numbered paragraph 8. However, to avoid complicating the exposition, I use the term "stimulation source," until numbered paragraph 8, to cover any or all of these meanings.)

(4) Two stimulation sources which are exactly similar – even a *single* stimulation source – may affect different organisms quite differently, of course. Indeed, a stimulation source which elicits *vitalizing* stimulation in an organism having *certain* properties may elicit *devitalizing* stimulation in an organism having *certain other* properties. Thus, for example, heat of a certain temperature may be vitalizing to *one* organism, devitalizing to *another*. Furthermore, though stimulation of a *certain* intensity (strength) may be *vitalizing* to an organism, stimulation of a *different* intensity (strength) may be *devitalizing* to that organism. Thus the stimulation elicited by heat of a *certain* temperature may be *vitalizing* to an organism but the stimulation elicited by heat of a *different* (considerably higher or considerably lower) temperature may be *devitalizing* to that organism. Finally, in virtue of the multiplicity of its characteristics and/or potential relationships, one and the same stimulation source can, either successively or at the same time, be *both vitalizing and devitalizing* to an organism (see numbered paragraph 12 below).

(5) When an organism responds so as to maximize stimulation from a given source (e.g., when a plant turns toward the sunlight or an animal attends to a certain sound or a person moves toward an attractive sex object), I shall call the response a "positive" one, positive, that is, in relation to that stimulation and that source. When it responds so as to

minimize stimulation from a given source (e.g., when antibodies combat bacteria or when an animal flees from danger or when a human being represses a painful recollection), I shall call the response a "negative" one, negative, that is, in relation to that stimulation and that source. When, in the absence of organically or traumatically induced pathology, an organism makes a *positive* form of response to a given stimulation source, it is reasonable to infer that it is receiving *vitalizing* stimulation from it. And when, in the absence of such pathology, an organism makes a *negative* form of response to a given source, it is reasonable to infer that it is receiving *devitalizing* stimulation from it. Given, in addition, certain information relating to the *level* of stimulation, it is also reasonable to make the *converse* inferences.

(6) A response which is in accordance with the BT – more precisely, which is in accordance with the relationship set forth in my statement of the BT – whether, in relation to a given stimulation source, it is positive or negative, is one which tends to increase or maintain the *internal well-being* or, as I shall often say, the *vitalization level* of the organism. This in turn tends to achieve the *preservation,* the *survival,* of the organism. In my view, self-preservation is brought about, not by the operation of a self-preservative "instinct" or "need" or "drive," at least if such an entity is conceived to be some sort of internal propelling force or psychical dynamism, but rather by behavior which conforms with my statement of the BT plus, it is important to add, a favorable set of circumstances. Obviously, the operation of the BT – like the alleged operation of a self-preservative "instinct" or "need" or "drive" – does not *assure* an organism's survival, or even the maintenance of its present level of vitalization, since some destructive factor, originating internally or externally, may intervene at any moment.[3]

(7) Stimulation is a physical process which in Man, and presumably in various other relatively "advanced" species,

may give rise to what I call "stimulation indicators" or, more briefly, "indicators," that is, to the *subjective components of sensory experiences* – specifically, the subjective components of sights, sounds, odors, tastes, tactile sensations, other bodily sensations (this is a somewhat heterogeneous group including, e.g., thermal sensations, kinesthetic sensations and various types of affect) and images. Stimulation indicators are not in physical, that is to say public, space-time and hence are "non-physical" or "psychical," terms which I use interchangeably.[4] Stimulation indicators may acquire, through a process of learning, structure (patternization) and various kinds and levels of "meaning". Somewhat comparable terms, as other writers have employed them, are: "directly experienced data," "representations," "sense data," "cues," etc. I prefer the term "stimulation indicators," among other reasons, because it points up what I regard as their primary biological and evolutionary function.[5]

(8) A stimulation indicator normally provides information (or the basis for "inferring" information) about a stimulation source (or about the internal condition, or about the external stimulus object, in which that source resides), including the relationship of that source (or condition or object) to the organism itself. A "stimulation source" may be either internal (inhering, e.g., in hunger contractions or in a state of exhaustion or in a bodily movement) or external. I shall sometimes have occasion to distinguish between an external source of stimulation and the physical object of which that stimulation source may be a part, calling the latter a "stimulus object." Thus as I sit here and look at my piano, that part of the chair's surface which is now touching me, as well as that part of the piano's surface which is now facing me, is a "stimulation source", but the chair itself, as well as the piano itself, is a "stimulus object." (In other words, the "stimulation source" is the *operative segment* of the stimulus object. Similarly with regard to the aforementioned internal condition; the "stimulation source" is, strictly speaking, the

operative segment of such a condition.) A stimulation source is to be distinguished from a "stimulus", though in many cases they are denotatively identical. In the instance just cited, the external "stimuli" include that part of the surface of the chair on which I am sitting and, not that part of the surface of the piano which is facing me, which is a stimulation source, but rather the retina-impinging stream of light waves coming from that source. For a "stimulus," as used here, is what *directly,* rather than *indirectly,* elicits stimulation. My use of the convenient term "stimulus situation" will, I think, be self-explanatory.

(9) The term "response" is employed in its broad biological sense to cover any functional modification *of* a living substance occurring in virtue of its properties *as* a living substance. In the so-called "higher" organisms, a response which is mediated by the nervous system characteristically entails an alteration in the action of either a muscle or a gland or both. *It should be borne in mind that a response itself, even an extremely minimal or incipient response (including, of course, the "thought" of making a response), concurrently elicits further stimulation.* (A response may or may not entail the occurrence of a stimulation indicator and hence of something "psychical.")

(10) I have stated the BT in terms of maximizing or minimizing *stimulation.* This is clearly preferable to stating it, for example, in terms of maximizing or minimizing a *stimulation source* or a *stimulus object* since the source or object may not itself be affected by the positive or negative response, e.g., by moving toward it or moving away from it; only its relationship to, and hence its effect upon, the organism may be altered by the response. A much less objectionable alternative would be to speak of maximizing or minimizing a *stimulus.* But, very strictly speaking, the stimulus itself (for example, a set of light waves) is not maximized or minimized by a response; it is rather that, as a result of a positive or negative response, one stimulus may

be replaced by another stimulus, for example, by one operating upon a larger or smaller body surface area or by one having a greater or lesser intensity. Moreover, very strictly speaking, it is the stimulation rather than the stimulus which actually *precipitates* the response. Nevertheless, when stimulation is being maximized or minimized by a response, it is necessarily true that, *in a sense,* the stimulus eliciting that stimulation is also being maximized or minimized by that response.

(11) In my statement of the BT, "maximizing" or "minimizing" stimulation has been partially equated with "increasing" or "decreasing" stimulation. In this connection I may also speak of "greater" or "lesser" stimulation. But where my emphasis is on the amount of stimulation received *within a given unit of time* (or other measuring unit), I am apt to speak of "more intense" or "less intense" stimulation or of "stronger" or "weaker" stimulation. (See numbered paragraph 4 of this Section.) Just what impact a particular stimulus will have is a function, of course, not only of the nature (including the location and duration) of the stimulus itself but also of the nature of the responding organism, including the "meaning" which that organism may attach to the related stimulation indicators. Thus an objectively weak stimulus, or rather stimulation source, such as a whisper or the rustling of a leaf, may, in virtue of its "meaning," set up very potent, even overwhelming, stimulation. If we should wish to *measure* the amount of stimulation evoked by a given stimulus we may do so either relatively *directly*, by noting certain *internal changes* (electrical, biochemical or physiological) or relatively *indirectly*, by observing certain aspects of the organism's *overt behavior*. On the behavioral level, for example, we may want to define the degree or the amount of the stimulation evoked by a given stimulus in terms of the range, vigor and persistence of the overt responses that stimulation seemingly elicits, modifies or inhibits.

(12) The stimulation evoked by a particular stimulation source in a particular organism can be both vitalizing and devitalizing, either successively or at the same time. In virtue of *some* of the characteristics of the stimulation source or stimulus object (or its operation upon an organism from a *certain* point in space or for a *certain* period of time), the stimulation may be vitalizing; in virtue of certain *other* of its characteristics (or its operation upon that organism from a *different* point in space or for a *different* period of time), the stimulation may be devitalizing. Thus someone may appear sexually attractive when seen at a distance but sexually unattractive when seen up close; sunlight may at first warm but later burn; food may be nourishing but at the same time be repulsive in odor; resting during a flight from danger may be reviving but at the same time create fear; an enemy may be a potential source of food but at the same time be a threat to survival. *When stimulation from a given source activates at the same time both a maximizing and a minimizing response (or any other incompatible responses) toward that source, we have conflict.* (We may also have conflict where a response tendency encounters, not an incompatible response tendency, but some thwarting situation.)[6] Let me add that since a living organism is a functional unit which embraces various *subordinate* functional units, *some* of its units may be engaged in maximizing what is vitalizing while *other* of its units are engaged in minimizing what is devitalizing.

(13) At any given moment, an organism is likely to be subjected to stimulation emanating from a variety of sources, both internal and external, and not infrequently special internal-external "partnerships" are formed. Suppose, e.g., that devitalizing stimulation is being evoked by a state of food deficiency and that this stimulation is giving rise to a sensation (stimulation indicator) of hunger. Here, as in the case of an external source of devitalizing stimulation, an organism tends to respond so as to get away from, or other-

wise reduce the impact of, the stimulation source. (Academic psychologists speak in this connection of the operation of "needs" or "drives.")[7] Since the source is internal, however, getting away from it in a literal, spatial sense is, of course, impossible. But it is significant that sooner or later there is apt to be a moving *toward something else*, specifically, *toward some food object*. Such a movement, if initially perhaps somewhat vascillating and uncertain—I am speaking here primarily of the behavior of creatures living in a "state of nature" — is apt to become quite rapid and direct once the food object is discovered. In other words, with the sudden increase in vitalizing stimulation, there is a sudden increase in maximization.

(14) In my statement of the BT I have spoken of a "direct relationship" — I am *not* claiming that the relationship is so invariant as to be reducible to a mathematical formula — between the degree of maximization and the degree to which stimulation is vitalizing and between the degree of minimization and the degree to which stimulation is devitalizing. To illustrate this further. If food is perceived by an animal which is *very* hungry, it tends to move toward that food, and to eat it, *more* rapidly than it would if it were *less* hungry. And if a situation confronting an animal is *very* frightening, it tends to turn away from, and to escape from, that situation *more* rapidly than it would if it were *less* frightened. Again, if an object one comes across is, for some reason or other, *very* attractive (*very* vitalizing), one tends to approach it *more* rapidly than one would if it were *less* attractive (*less* vitalizing); and if it is *very* repulsive (*very* devitalizing), one tends to move away from it *more* rapidly than one would if it were *less* repulsive (*less* devitalizing).[8] *Thus the operation of the Basic Tendency is analogous to the operation of an air cooling system (though an air cooling system which functions somewhat imperfectly) which sucks in (maximizes) cool air (vitalizing stimulation) with a degree of vigor which increases as the temperature of the outside*

air drops (becomes more vitalizing) and which shuts out (minimizes) warm air (devitalizing stimulation) with a degree of vigor which increases as the temperature of the outside air rises (becomes more devitalizing).

Of course there are *limits* to the degree to which an organism (or an air cooling system) can maximize or minimize stimulation, limits which are imposed by the nature and condition of that organism. Thus an animal can move toward, or move away from, a stimulation source only up to a certain maximal speed; and if, let us say, it has been injured, it may not be able to move at all. Such limitations aside, however, a direct relationship between the variables in question is clearly present.

1. See the Sections, "The Basic Tendency Versus Other Life-Principles," pp. 22-24, and "Instinct and the BT," pp. 39-40.
2. See the Section, "The Genesis of Psychopathology," pp. 160-164.
3. See the Section, "Self-Destructive Behavior," pp. 142-143.
4. See the Section, "Metaphysical Dualism," pp. 56-61. By the term "stimulation indicator," I mean either the *whole* of my visual or auditory or olfactory, etc. field of experience or *any segment* of it.
5. See the Section, "The Evolutionary Emergence of Stimulation Indicators," pp. 48-49.
6. See the Section, "The Genesis of Psychopathology," pp. 161-163.
7. For comments on this view, see the Section, "Needs, Drives and the BT", pp. 42-44.
8. With regard to the relationship implied here between positive and negative affect and vitalizing and devitalizing stimulation, see the Section, "A Related Principle Concerning Affect," pp. 18-19.

THE BASIC FORMS OF RESPONSE

If we take an overall look at the behavior of living organisms, from the blue-green algae or the amoeba, on the one hand, to homo sapiens, on the other, we find that maximizing and minimizing responses, though remarkably varied, fall readily into certain basic patterns, patterns which are at once mutually exclusive (i.e., non-overlapping) and all-inclusive (i.e., exhaust all the theoretical possibilities). Let us consider first the basic ways of maximizing vitalizing stimulation.

Here the most extensively employed means is some form of *absorption* or *incorporation*. In fact, absorption or incorporation is a capacity possessed in some degree by *all* living organisms. The specific character of the substance which is taken in may be quite different in different instances, of course, ranging, for example, from sunlight or water or air to highly complex organic compounds. And the nature, and the degree of complexity, of the biochemical transformation process required for the utilization of what is absorbed or incorporated may also vary greatly. Initially limited in their employment of this form of response, organisms in the course of evolution expanded and refined their incorporating ability. In addition, they acquired and then increased the capacity to *store* or *preserve* sources of vitalizing stimulation, thus being able to avail themselves of such sources (e.g., in the form of a reserve internal or external food supply) at some future date.

The capacity to *turn toward* a source of vitalization and the further capacity to *move toward* (including the capacity to *move into*) a source of vitalization represented the development of two additional means of maximizing vitalizing stimulation. Both forms of response fall within the repertoire of most species of animals. In plants, typically unable to engage in any kind of overall locomotion, the turning toward response is perhaps particularly striking in the ability of certain vascular species to react phototropistically.

With respect to the basic ways of minimizing devitalizing stimulation, we may say that these are, in somewhat different senses, the "opposite" of the maximizing ways we have just enumerated. Thus in contrast to *absorption* or *incorporation,* we have *exclusion* (including *ejection*); in contrast to *storage* or *preservation,* we have partial or total *destruction* (that is, the changing of a source of devitalizing stimulation so as to render it less devitalizing);[1] and in contrast to turning *toward* or to moving *toward* (including moving *into*), we have turning *away from* or moving *away from* (including moving *out of*) – in other words, *withdrawing from.* These negative responses may be divided still more simply into those by which an organism diminishes (that is, partially or totally destroys) the stimulation source itself and those by which an organism merely diminishes the stimulation which it receives from that source (as in excluding, in turning away from, or in moving away from).[2]

It should be noted that the basic forms of maximizing and minimizing response which have been enumerated have applicability not only to an organism *as a whole* but also to its *subordinate functional units,* for example, to individual cells or to groups of coordinated cells – to the action of viruses or of antibodies, to the formation of protective scabs, to the body's rejection or acceptance of transplants, etc. It should also be noted that in Man, and doubtless in other "higher" organisms too, the basic forms of maximizing and minimizing response are employed, not only on various *physiological* or *physical* levels, but on various *psychological* levels as well. Thus there is an obvious legitimacy in regarding learning, e.g., as a form of absorbing or incorporating, remembering, e.g., as a form of storing or preserving, investigating, e.g., as a form of turning toward or moving toward, repressing, e.g., as a form of excluding, verbally attacking, e.g., as a form of destroying and emotionally withdrawing, e.g., as a form of turning away or moving away. Further references to the operation of the BT on the psychological level are made in later Sections.[3] I would also suggest that there is a significant degree of correspondence between the three basic forms of positive response, namely, absorbing or incorporating, storing or preserving and turning toward or moving toward and the three basic types of personality orientation, namely, the oral, the anal and the phallic (or genital) which are described by Freud.[4]

Let us now return to our statement of the BT and to its implicit classification of organic responses into those which are positive (maximizing) and those which are negative (minimizing). *If we allow ourselves to speak metaphorically, we may say that the BT implies the operation of a Fusion Principle and a Separation Principle in all living organisms.* So far as an organism is responding positively, is seeking to increase contact with what is vitalizing, the Fusion Principle may be said to be manifesting itself. So far as an organism is responding negatively, is seeking to decrease contact with what is devitalizing, the Separation Principle may be said to be manifesting itself.[5] With more subjectivism, and in the fashion of Empedocles, we might call these the Love and Hate Principles. (Compare Freud's Life and Death instincts.) I should like to emphasize, however, that, for the present at least, I regard these so-called "Principles" merely as *as-if* entities and thus as devoid of any ontological reality.[6]

1. A destructive end *can* be achieved by means of absorption or incorporation. Thus absorption or incorporation is a reponse (or a series of responses) which *can* serve (though it *need not* serve) a *double* function, that of *maximizing* the *vitalizing* stimulation produced by something's *life-serving* aspect and that of *minimizing* the *devitalizing* stimulation produced

by its *life-endangering* aspect. (In this connection, see the preceding Section, numbered paragraph 12.)

2. A negative response, that is, a response directed toward minimizing the DV stimulation evoked by a given source, may involve a *preparatory* response which is *positive.* If, for example, one animal attacks another, attending to, moving toward and other positive responses may occur first. These responses, however, are incidental to the major response which is *negative.* On the psychological level, the situation is somewhat similar to reviewing some disturbing situation so as to be able to "put it out of one's mind".

3. See, among other Sections, "Needs, Drives and the BT," pp. 42-44, "Dreams and the BT," pp. 118-121, "Some Miscellaneous Vitalization Patterns," pp. 140-141, "The Defense Mechanisms," pp. 147-148 and "Vitalistic Psychotherapy," pp. 166-172.

4. It should be noted that for Freud the oral, the anal and the phallic (genital) are concepts applicable to Man rather than to *all* species of organisms and that they relate to the role of *special organs* of the human body, namely, the mouth, the anus and the genitalia, rather than to other parts of the human body or to the human body as a whole. The emphasis on these special organs as vehicles of "libidinal gratification" serves to narrow these Freudian concepts still further. I would like to suggest (a) that Freud overlooked the fact that throughout the organic world there are three fundamental and universal types of positive response, namely absorbing (incorporating), storing (preserving) and turning toward or moving toward (including moving into) and (b) that "oral incorporation", "anal retention" and "genital sexuality" are, respectively, merely particular (i.e., humanized, localized and libidinized) examples of these basic forms.

5. See the Section, "Fusion and Separation in Relation to World History," pp. 83-86.

6. See the Section, "The Definition of Existence and Reality," pp. 74-77.

THE VITALIZING EFFECT OF STIMULATION PER SE

I believe there is a good reason to assume (and I shall accordingly do so)[1] that *in human beings and in many, perhaps all, other species of organisms, stimulation as such (that is, regardless of whether its predominant effect is vitalizing or devitalizing) tends to have*[2] *in some respect a vitalizing effect and, up to a limiting point, to have this effect (other characteristics of the stimulation being unchanged) in direct relationship to its strength or intensity.*[3]

I would like to suggest that it is this relationship between stimulation and vitalization which, in conjunction with the operation of the BT, serves to bring about, among other phenomena, the following:

(1) the occurrence of "exploratory" behavior, that is, behavior involving the moving toward and/or the investigation of one's sensory (or ideational) environment. Such behavior has often been attributed by psychologists to the operation of an exploratory "instinct" or "need" or "drive". But if, as I am here asserting, stimulation *as such* tends to be vitalizing and if, as the BT formula states, vitalization tends to induce maximization, this form of behavior is just what, at least in the absence of counteracting factors, we might anticipate.

(2) the marked, almost compelling, tendency in Man, and in various other species, to focus attention on that part of the stimulus situation which at the moment is eliciting particularly strong (intense) stimulation — for example, an unexpected stirring in the underbrush, a loud sound, a sharp pain, an exciting fantasy, etc.[4] Focusing one's attention on some element is, let me point out, a way of *maximizing* the

induced stimulation, a way of "opening oneself up" to that stimulation more fully. Thus when, in virtue of the unusual intensity of the stimulation induced by some element in the stimulus situation, that stimulation is, for the instant, highly vitalizing (whatever devitalizing effect it may also have), some maximizing response to that element – and attention giving is, in a sense, a very *fundamental* maximizing response – is virtually automatic.[5]

I have said that the direct relationship in question tends to be present "up to a limiting point" (see the first sentence in this Section). Thus the increasing intensity of the stimulation induced in an animal by the approach of a fearsome enemy or, in the case of Man, by the "approach" of a fearsome future event, may at some point *cease* to have an increasingly vitalizing effect – indeed at some point the increasing intensity of the stimulation may actually produce a predominantly devitalizing and even paralyzing effect.[6]

1. That a lack of stimulation may adversely affect an organism's functioning is a conclusion which appears to gain support from a diversity of studies. In addition to various biological studies, see, e.g., the child nurturing studies of Margaretha Ribble and Rene Spitz and the neurophysiological studies of D.O. Hebb and J. C. Lilly.

2. That is, given the presence of sufficient stimulation, *does* have in the absence of organically or traumatically induced pathology.

3. Though I am speaking here primarily of organisms as *wholes* or *totalities*, in a number of instances my statement also has applicability to the subordinate functional units of organisms.

4. Since stimulation inducing an "emotional" response (fear, anger, sexual arousal, joy, etc.) is apt to be quite strong, it is apt to have a significant vitalizing effect, whatever devitalizing effect (as in the case of fear or anger) it also may have.

5. It is frequently maintained that a child tends to "identify" with the "stronger" of his two parents. What takes place in connection with such identification is doubtless a complicated process which varies considerably from one instance to another. But I would like to propose that the process is rooted in our compelling tendency to maximize what is providing very strong stimulation.

6. See the Section, "The Genesis of Psychopathology," pp. 160-164.

A RELATED PRINCIPLE CONCERNING AFFECT

Let me now state a principle which bears a significant relationship to the BT. This principle is that *in human beings, and presumably in many other species of organisms, vitalizing stimulation tends to evoke*[1] *hedonically positive affect and devitalizing stimulation tends to evoke hedonically negative affect.*[2] In other words, vitalizing or devitalizing stimulation tends to induce, respectively, a pleasing or displeasing feeling.[3]

The pleasingness or displeasingness which is felt is, of course, "subjective",[4] that is to say, it is a *private* phenomenon and is not actually inherent in (is not literally a part of) the stimulus object (or internal condition) which serves to activate it. Like any other stimulation indicator, however, it tends to be projected. (This fact is pertinent to my statement of a "pleasure-pain principle" in the Section which follows.) Thus when someone experiences a hedonically positive (pleasing) or a hedonically negative (displeasing) feeling, he is apt to perceive it (at least after a period of learning) as being "attached" to the stimulus object (or internal condition) which is eliciting the V or DV stimulation. Note, for example, that when we have a positive (or negative) feeling in connection with drinking a cup of coffee, or in connection with being in the company of a certain person, we are likely to comment favorably (or unfavorably) on *its* or on *his* pleasing (or displeasing) qualities. Under other circumstances, however, positive or negative affect may be felt to be more or less diffuse or free-floating; in other words, there may be little or no projection on to any *specific* stimulus object (or internal condition).

The process by which positive or negative affect comes to

be linked with (projected upon) a stimulus object (or internal condition) which did not *previously* evoke it, or evoke it in its present form, may be viewed as constituting a very basic type of "transference". It is a process which is subject, of course, to the effects of learning.[5]

1. That is, given a sufficient increment of increase, *does* evoke in the absence of organically or traumatically induced pathology. See the Section, "The Genesis of Psychopathology," pp. 160-164.

2. I am speaking here, of course, only of organisms as *wholes* or *totalities,* not of the subordinate functional units of organisms, since I presume, as most persons do, that only organisms as wholes or totalities may experience feelings. This limitation also applies to the derivative principles set forth in the following Section.

3. One is tempted to add that, up to a limiting point, there is a "direct relationship" between the variables in question, that is to say, that as the first variable increases so does the second. But such a statement presupposes that pleasing or displeasing feelings (affect) fall unequivocally into a single order or hierarchy, like the numbers 1, 2, 3 and 4. This, however, is not the case. The fact that there may be a difference in the *quality* of the "pleasingness" characterizing two pleasing feelings nullifies the possibility of rating their "pleasingness" in purely quantitative terms.

4. See the Section, "Metaphysical Dualism," pp. 56-61.

5. So too, no doubt, though in a quite different way, is what I would call the "primary" projective process, that is, the process whereby the very young infant comes to perceive sensory data (stimulation indicators) as having definite positions "out there" in space.

DERIVATIVE PRINCIPLES

I now want to state a third principle which is derived from the first two, that is, from the principle concerning the BT and from the related principle just mentioned. This derivative principle is that *in human beings, and presumably in many other species of organisms, there is a tendency to respond so as to maximize stimulation which tends to evoke hedonically positive (i.e., pleasing) affect and so as to minimize stimulation which tends to evoke hedonically negative (i.e., displeasing) affect.* Now if we relate this principle to what was said in the preceding Section regarding the projection of positive or negative affect on to the stimulus object (or internal condition) inducing it, we can arrive at this *further* principle, namely, that *in human beings, and presumably in many other species of organisms, there is a tendency to respond so as to maximize stimulation which tends to lead to the perception of the stimulus object (or internal condition) as hedonically positive and so as to minimize stimulation which tends to lead to the perception of such an object (or condition) as hedonically negative.* Stated very briefly, if somewhat less exactly, *there is a tendency to maximize what is perceived (felt) as pleasing and to minimize what is perceived (felt) as displeasing.*

In the light of what has been said, it is clear that *this fourth or "pleasure-pain" principle, as it may be called, is not at all a basic principle – as Freud, for example, considered such a principle to be – but rather a derivative principle, one resting in part, moreover, on the BT.*

THE BASIC TENDENCY VERSUS OTHER LIFE-PRINCIPLES

When I am feeling rather pleased with myself, I am inclined to believe that my statement of the BT represents the first formulation, in a sense, the discovery, of the most fundamental principle governing the behavior of living organisms. It is a principle which, as I see it, has heretofore been conceived, if indeed it can be said to have been conceived at all, only *very vaguely,* in terms of some kind of transcendent and ubiquitous instinct or need or drive or vital force, etc. which somehow brings about the preservation or survival of organisms, or *very incompletely,* in terms of so-called "adient" (toward) and "avoidant" (away from) drives, or "adient" and "avoidant" responses,[1] drives and responses, however, which, in addition to having been given only a limited area of application, have been left completely unrelated to the maximization of vitalizing, and the minimization of devitalizing, stimulation.

I should like to make a few brief comments here – though in view of their brevity, I am afraid they will necessarily seem to be dogmatic – by way of comparing (my statement of) the BT with certain other broad hypotheses concerning the behavior of living organisms. The comparison will be with other comprehensive, unitary (single) principles, allegedly falling within the framework of science rather than of religion or metaphysics, which have been presented as having explanatory relevance to organismic behavior in general. These principles would seem to be of three major types: (a) life-principles concerning the (guiding) role of some subjective factor, most commonly a feeling of pleasure (or freedom from pain) or a feeling of well-being; (b) life-principles concerning the (propelling) role of some ubiquitous instinct or need or drive or vital force, etc., most commonly in the direction of self-preservation or survival; (c) life-principles concerning the (stabilizing) role of some intra-organismic regulatory factor, such as homeostasis. In my judgment, however, these alternative life-principles, at least so far as they may be alleged to be *primary* life-principles, have significant limitations.

(a) With regard to hypotheses stated in terms of the role of some subjective factor, such as a feeling of pleasure or a feeling of well-being, one may make at least two quite obvious points: (1) that the presence of such subjective states, except perhaps where human introspection is possible, is unverifiable by any form of direct observation and is of necessity, therefore, a matter of conjecture; (2) that, as a matter of fact, such subjective concepts are only rarely even *presumed* to be applicable to the less "advanced" forms of life (for example, to plants) or to *any* organism's subordinate physiological units – say, to its individual cells.

(b) If we turn to hypotheses stated in terms of the role of some ubiquitous instinct or need or drive or vital force, etc., there are other difficulties which we confront. (1) For one thing, if such an entity exists, its existence can account at best only for the *general direction* which organic responses take, not for any of the *specific inter-relationships* they manifest. For as such an entity is usually conceived, it is without any discrete, much less quantitative, characteristics. (2) Even in this regard, however, this type of view is, in my judgment, unsatisfactory. For although such an entity presumably has observable consequences, it itself is admittedly unobservable. This, per se, is unobjectionable; science, of course, is constantly positing the existence of transcendent entities. But in this instance as, e.g., in the case of the Ether, there is no *independent* evidence other than that which the hypothesized entity (i.e., the ubiquitous instinct or need, etc.) is specifically designed to "explain".[2] Thus the so-called "explanation" offered by this type of view is nominal (verbal) rather than real.[3] *In contrast, my statement of the BT is an assertion of a relationship between entities both of which are observable;* specifically, it is an assertion of a co-variant form of relationship between a vitalizing effect, on the one hand, and a maximizing response, on the other, and between a devitalizing effect, on the one hand, and a minimizing response, on the other. It should also be noted – and this is a point of equal importance – that *the BT offers an explanation of organic behavior which is completely non-teleological.*

(c) An increasing amount of attention has been given in recent years to various physiological and behavioral *regulatory* mechanisms, with the result that there have emerged a number of comprehensive regulatory concepts. Though certain writers have placed particular emphasis on the "integrative" or "organizing" functions of an organism, it is probably the concept of "homeostasis" – that is, the concept that an organism tends to maintain or restore a state of internal equilibrium – which, in one form or another, is the most widely employed regulatory concept. I have no wish to question the usefulness of the concept of homeostasis[4], or any other such regulatory concept, so long as we recognize that it can provide us only with a *descriptive framework* for the bodily processes in question, not with a *basic explanation* of those processes. Presented as a primary life-principle, such a concept is quite inadequate. For it leaves completely unanswered the question: *why* (i.e., in accordance with what *more general* principle) do the responses of an organism tend to bring about *one* particular state, namely, a state of internal equilibrium, rather than some *other* state? To answer *this* question requires reference, as I see it, to the matter of *vitalization* and hence brings us back to the BT. My answer would be: so far as an organism *does* respond in a manner which tends to bring about a certain state (for example, homeostasis), *it does so because such a state is the result of responses which are in accord with the BT. Thus homeostasis, or any other regulatory principle, is at best a secondary or derivative life-principle, not a primary one.*

Let me add one or two observations concerning a conceptualization of behavior which may be regarded as employing a *special form* of the homeostatic principle. In current experimental studies of animal and human behavior, the factor which activates behavior is quite commonly viewed as a "tension" stimulus (drive, etc.) which the organism seeks to remove. The position is that when, for example, a hunger stimulus (drive, etc.) or a sex stimulus (drive, etc.) is present, this activates (motivates) the subject into undertaking a response, or series of responses, which will have the result, or at least the postulated aim, of eliminating that tension stimulus and thus of restoring a state of non-tension.

But implicit in this view is the assumption that all stimuli (drives, etc.) have a *negative* (frustrating, annoying, etc.) quality and on the surface, at least, this assumption does not jibe with the facts. Thus, for example, when a cat or a dog (not to mention a human being!) is gently stroked, it will often make a response which, instead of serving to reduce or eliminate the stroking, will serve to maintain or increase it. Now it is possible to reply to this objection by arguing that the stimulus (drive, etc.) here is not the stroking, but the activated *hunger* for stroking which, like the hunger for food, is a tension stimulus (drive, etc.) and hence one which the organism will seek to reduce or eliminate. This answer, however, appears to me to be grossly artificial, for the fact remains that in some instances the organism tends to *decrease* or to *terminate* the stimulation it is receiving and in some instances to *maintain* or to *increase* that stimulation. In other words, in some instances it tends to respond *negatively* and in some instances, *positively. The tension-reduction view either ignores, or fails to do justice to, this very basic behavioral fact.*

1. See Holt, Edwin B., *Animal Drive and the Learning Process,* New York: Holt, 1931.

2. For additional comments on "explaining" behavior, see the Section, "Instinct and the BT," pp. 39-40.

3. An "operational" definition of such an instinct or need, etc. is not feasible. Since that instinct or need, etc. is, by hypothesis, *ubiquitous* — that is, *omnipresent* — it is impossible to equate or correlate it with any *particular* set of observable data, as it is, for example, in relation to a *specific* need such as the need for food. The latter can be operationally defined, e.g., in terms of food deprivation over a given period of time. In this connection, see the Section, "Needs, Drives and the BT," pp. 42-43.

4. Nor, for that matter, the concept of "heterostasis".

SCIENTIFIC HYPOTHESIS AND THE BT

A scientific hypothesis sets forth a relationship which is, or at least can be, stated in the form: if such-and-such is the case, then such-and-such else will also be the case. The *statement* of the relationship must be distinguished, of course, from the *relationship itself,* just as the *relationship itself* must be distinguished from a particular *instance* of that relationship.

My statement of the BT is a statement of a specified relationship between the occurrence of vitalizing or devitalizing stimulation and the occurrence of a maximizing or minimizing response. Let me compare it, for a moment, though it may seem presumptuous to do so, with, say, Newton's law (that is, *statement*) in regard to gravitation.

Given certain conditions, a physical body falling toward the Earth will accelerate its speed in accordance with the Newtonian formula. Only the presence of some interfering factor (e.g., wind resistance or the impact of some other body) will prevent the falling object from fully obeying the Newtonian law (formula). If we consider the response of an organism to vitalizing or devitalizing stimulation, we find that the situation is essentially similar. Here the relevant formula is the relationship specified in my statement of the Basic Tendency. And here it is only the presence of the limiting conditions noted which will prevent an organism from fully complying with the BT formula.

Both the Newtonian formula and the BT formula are applicable to an extremely broad range of well-defined entities. The Newtonian formula applies to any physical body which is in a state of free suspension, the BT formula, to any living organism (at least to any of which we know) which is free from organically or traumatically induced pathology and which is subjected to stimulation falling within a certain intensity range. It needs to be remembered that the universality of the BT formula is in no way compromised by the fact that one living organism may maximize or minimize stimulation in a different manner (form) or at a different speed or with a different degree of effectiveness than some other living organism.

Both the Newtonian formula and the BT formula permit us to make verifiable predictions. In the latter case, however, it is understandably more difficult to state those predictions with exactitude. For one thing, it is probably more difficult to ascertain, and hence to calibrate, degrees of vitalization or devitalization and degrees of maximization or minimization than it is to ascertain and calibrate masses, distances and accelerations. Moreover, the formula set forth in my statement of the BT specifies a *direct* relationship but not one which is so fixed and unvarying as to be expressible in *mathematical* terms.

PART TWO

SOME SPECULATIONS AND APPLICATIONS

SPECULATIONS ON THE BEGINNING OF LIFE

I would like to offer some thoughts, admittedly highly speculative, in regard to how the evolutionary process may have gotten under way. I do so with full awareness of my limited knowledge of biological theory and of biological fact, yet not without a modicum of hope, I confess, that my hypothesis will be found, at the least, to be provocative. After all, when it comes to the origin of life, none of us can claim to be an "expert", in the full sense of that term.

In order to point up the distinguishing features of my hypothesis, let me compare it with the view which prevails in biological circles today, a view set forth, for example, in the contemporary classic, *Your Heredity and Environment* (J. P. Lippincott Co., 1965), written by my friend, Amram Scheinfeld. I quote this significant passage (pp. 562-563):

> "Finally, after eons of such events, the gap was bridged between the non-living and the living with the appearance of a bit of substance that in some way could reproduce itself. It may have resembled a segment of the DNA – that is, consisting of a few links of adenine and thymine, cysposine and quanine, forming a simple AT,TA,CG,GC... coded arrangement. Here, in effect, we had a "gene" able to transmit a coded message. When a number of such genes combined and worked together – forming a chromosome – they were able eventually to surround themselves with a globule of the life stuff protoplasm within which they could operate and have their instructions carried out. The result now was a *living* cell and at once this cell began to exercise the unique power given it by its genes to reproduce

itself endlessly until there were countless other one-cell organisms."

Now it seems to me highly unlikely that, as asserted in the first sentence of this passage, the first bit of living substance did have the capacity to reproduce itself. And it seems to me still more unlikely that this was a capacity for some (elementary or partial) form of *genetic* reproduction. For *genetic* reproduction, certainly as it is manifest today in even the simplest living substance, is an amazingly complex and intricate process entailing an extremely high degree of specialization, differentiation and interdependence of function, the details of which process still lie beyond both our observation and our understanding.

In contrast to the view summarized in this passage, it would be my hypothesis that the first bits of living substance, having only a relatively simple structure and a very limited ability to maintain themselves, almost certainly died "childless". At some point, however, some of the globules being formed must have been able to respond to a significant degree in accordance with the Basic Tendency and it was at this point, we might say, that the evolutionary process was effectively initiated. For possessing this capacity, they would now have the potential, probably through a process of physicochemical absorption, not only to prolong their aliveness (i.e., sustain their vitalization level), but also to expand or grow. Other things being equal, those bits of living matter which happened to be in a more favorable environment would achieve these ends, of course, more successfully.

It would be my supposition that it was this growth or expansion through absorption which provided the basis for the first rudimentary (non-genetic) form of reproduction. I would suggest that the process of absorption, or incorporation, increased the internal pressure against the (physicochemical) forces operating to contain the living substance — to keep it united — and that when that pressure exceeded those forces, the substance split into separate parts. We may assume that those parts also functioned in accordance with the BT and thus that they too expanded and then fragmented.

Reproduction on a "bi-parental" basis may well have come about somewhat as follows. Two units of living matter, perhaps by chance, perhaps in accordance with the BT, may have in some degree merged or fused. Guided by the BT, the resulting substance could be expected to respond in a manner resembling that of its parental substances; in other words, it too could be expected to expand and then to break apart. And so the process of union (interpenetration) and fragmentation might continue from one generation to the next.

Whether or not a particular type of bi-parental reproduction can qualify as "sexual" reproduction depends, of course, on how we define the nature and the degree of the required difference between the parental units. It is certainly fair to assume, however, that, with the passage of time, the various units of living matter, including the parental units which were being merged, did become more and more differentiated so that, other things being equal, "sexual" reproduction became more and more likely.

In this type of bi-parental reproduction we have a primitive form of inheritance but a form in which there is as yet no role for genes or chromosomes. How did the genetic form of inheritance come about? How did genes and chromosomes come to exist? I repeat: I cannot believe that the extraordinarily complex set of operations involved in genetic inheritance was present, even in an elementary or partial form, at the outset of the evolutionary process. Rather, I would think that genes, and the processes to which they give rise, were the product of an extended *antecedent* evolutionary process.

Let us return to the simple form of bi-parental (sexual?) reproduction we have just mentioned, a form involving the fusion of two units of living substance and the subsequent fragmentation of the interpenetrated segment into separate units. Here we have inheritance but here the material in the interpenetrated area is a *sizable portion,* perhaps *even the whole,* of the material comprising the bodies of the two parents, not just a minute fraction of that parental material, as in genetic inheritance. How has this change in the process of heredity been brought about?

It seems to me reasonable to suppose that, as a result of the operation of the BT and of environmental (natural) selection, the parents of the fused material would gradually arrive at a more *economical* birth process, that is, one in which their contribution would be more and more limited to the essential birth ingredients. For a reduction in the loss of parental substance would help preserve the integrity and viability of the parents and at the same time increase their reproductive capacity. This essential birth material (rudimentary chromosomal material), like the parental substance, would absorb what was vitalizing to it, in accordance with the BT. And because of its being substantively derived from the parental material and its living in the same parental environment, we could expect it to give rise to mature organisms revealing a marked parental resemblance.

What I am suggesting here is the occurrence of a process which is roughly analogous to the deflation and inflation of a balloon – let us say, a balloon on which is imprinted in black outline a picture of Mickey Mouse. When the air is removed and the balloon crumples, all that visibly remains of that picture is a conglomeration of small, broken black lines (the genes). But when the balloon is re-inflated – let us say, with a somewhat different gas – the outline of a figure which closely resembles Mickey Mouse reappears.

In the light of this analogy, let me now briefly restate my genetic hypothesis as follows: *pre-genetic evolution involved a gradual and extended-over-many-generations process of "deflation" (or "condensation") whose residual ingredients (rudimentary genes), when "inflated," gave rise to parent resembling organisms.*

Though the hypothesis I am suggesting admittedly is highly speculative, I must note that I have looked in vain elsewhere for a more plausible alternative. Indeed the question as to how it is that genes have come to have the capacity to give rise to full fledged functioning organisms, to organisms, moreover, which are parent resembling, is a question which biologists rarely seem to have asked. The gene appears to be naively viewed as a kind of super-intelligent "agent" which somehow has received highly complicated secret "orders" which it then automatically and unerringly carries out. But genes are *not* agents endowed with super-intelligence or even with ordinary human intelligence, and no "orders" have been given to them. This is sheer metaphor – and unresolved mystery.

Although some of the principles of evolution – I have referred to natural selection and to the Basic Tendency – must have been operative *before* the emergence of genes, it was of course only *after* their emergence that *mutations* and *variations* could become generators of evolutionary change. But at this point we move beyond "the beginning of life" with less need, as well as less opportunity, perhaps, to engage in flights of fancy.

THE BT IN RELATION TO FERTILIZATION AND VARIATION

I would like to say something about the role of the BT in relation to two key biological processes, viz, fertilization and variation.

In regard to the process of fertilization, much is known, of course, about the conditions which must exist in order for it to be *possible* for fertilization to occur. Stated grossly, the recognized essential conditions normally are that the germ cells involved (a) be opposite-sexed representatives of the same species, (b) possess an adequate degree of vitality, and (c) come into appropriate physical contact with one another. But *I would suggest that the BT is also a factor here – that two opposite-sexed germ cells which have the capacity to vitalize each other to a greater degree than do two other opposite-sexed germ cells of that species are, other things being equal, more likely to unite with one another – that is, more likely to respond positively toward each other, to maximize each other, by moving toward and into one another.* Just as a mature organism tends to make a *more* positive response toward a *more* vitalizing stimulation source, so too, I would presume, does a germ cell. Thus when fertilization takes place with unaccountable ease or, for that matter, with unaccountable difficulty, the explanation may well lie, I would suggest, in the BT. Where there is unaccountable difficulty, for example, the germ cells involved simply may not possess the vitalizing properties needed to elicit vigorous positive responses from one another.

What has been said here in relation to fertilization applies also to the occurrence of variations or mutations. In other words, I would suggest that *there also is a selective process which operates in relation to the external influences which impinge upon genes and chromosomes, a tendency being present to make a maximizing response to vitalizing stimulation and a minimizing response to devitalizing stimulation.*

To be sure, genes and chromosomes are strongly *resistant* to environmental influence so that only quite *potent* forces (cosmic rays, X-rays, special chemical agents, etc.) are apt to bring about any internal structural or compositional changes.[1] It is my hypothesis, however, not that the BT is powerful enough, so to speak, to *reverse* this probability but merely that it tends in some degree to *modify* it – by maximizing the impact of what is vitalizing to the genes and chromosomes and minimizing the impact of what is devitalizing to them. It should be noted that by sustaining or raising the vitalization level (promoting the internal well-being) of the germ cells and their constituent genes and chromosomes, the BT *indirectly* is sustaining or raising the vitalization level of the developed (mature) organisms to which they give rise. *Thus in this way too the BT contributes towards the acceleration of the evolutionary process itself.*

There is one further point to be made regarding the relationship between the BT and genetic changes. And this is that *it is only in virtue of the BT that a potentially useful genetic change (variation or mutation) proves to be "favorable."* For it is only in virtue of the BT that the responses of an organism tend to promote its internal well-being and thus, indirectly, to aid its survival. *Without the BT, an organism would lack the propensity to utilize a "favorable" variation or mutation in its own self-interest.* Obviously any organism logically *could* use a "favorable" variation or mutation – one, say, making for greater strength or greater aggressivity or greater mobility, etc. – in a repeatedly *futile* or even in a repeatedly *self-destructive* way. Thus though the *occurrence* of "favorable" variations and mutations is of critical importance in the evolutionary process, so too is their *effective utilization.* And this points again to the significant role of the BT.

1. I would suggest that this fact is not unrelated to the fact that those external influences are more likely to be damaging than beneficent.

INSTINCT AND THE BT

(a) I have said in my statement of the Basic Tendency that a living organism tends to respond so as to maximize the vitalizing stimulation it receives and so as to minimize the devitalizing stimulation it receives – say, by turning in this direction rather than that or by absorbing this substance rather than that. But what may be highly vitalizing for one kind of organism, with one type of structure or composition, may, of course, be much less vitalizing, even devitalizing, for a different kind of organism, with a different type of structure or composition. Thus the BT may lead organisms of different species (not to mention different individuals within the *same* species) in quite different directions, so to speak. One species will build nests, another will burrow itself in the ground.

On my view what distinguishes one form from some other form of "instinctual" behavior is not the presence of a different psychical dynamism or propelling force of some kind but simply a difference in the form of the behavior itself. Each form of instinctual behavior, whether it be the absorption of sunlight by a plant or the flight of an animal in the face of danger or the combativeness of an animal in the face of territorial invasion or the nest building of a bird or the sexual behavior of Man, is merely a manifestation, in a different context – i.e., by a different bodily structure which is being subjected to a different set of stimuli – of the operation of the BT.[1]

(b) To call certain forms of behavior "instinctual," whether or not we *name* the so-called instinct, is to *label* the behavior but not, of course, thereby to *explain* it. For explanation commonly requires (that is, in virtue of what we usually *mean* by "explanation") that we be able to view what is being explained as a consequence – either logical or empirical – of something else. We must be able to point to a *hypothesis* from which what is to be explained can be *inferred* (deduced) or to a particular *cause* of which it is an *effect* (a result).

Thus the fact, e.g., that organisms tend to behave so as to preserve themselves is not explained by saying that the behavior is due to a self-preservative instinct – or, for that matter, to a self-preservative drive or need – at least if in saying this we are limiting ourselves to the verbal expression itself and are pointing neither to an implicative hypothesis nor to an operative, independently verifiable, cause. But if we bear in mind the statement of the BT, we see that we *do* have an implicative hypothesis on the basis of which self-preservative behavior *can* be explained. For we then recognize that maximizing vitalizing stimulation and minimizing devitalizing stimulation tends to raise or to maintain the vitalization level of the organism and that this in turn tends to make for, though of course it does not guarantee, the preservation of the organism.

The same comment applies if we should posit a sexual instinct or an aggressive instinct or a nest building instinct, etc. Unless we are pointing to an implicative hypothesis or to an operative, independently verifiable, cause, our "explanation" is purely verbal.[2] If we bear in mind, however, the operation of the BT, we *have* an explanation of these forms of behavior, for we then see that these forms of instinctual behavior are consequences of the BT – i.e., that they occur as a result of responses which are in conformity with it.

(c) The unfolding of an instinctual behavior pattern, particularly where the behavior is intricate and exquisitely adaptive, often evokes in the lay, and even the professional, observer a sense of wonder bordering on a sense of the uncanny. For it is as if the present somehow had been fully anticipated, as if the organism were playing a part which had been written for it long ago. In a manner of speaking, of course, this is true. But *the script was written, I should say, not by the recognized principles of evolution alone, but also by the BT.*[3] As to whether or not an appreciation of the contribution made by the BT would *reduce* that sense of wonder, I cannot say. Perhaps I should even be sorry if it did!

1. What is said here is equally applicable to the "reflex" behavior of an organism — e.g., the eye-blinking or sneezing reflex.

2. See the Section, "The Basic Tendency Versus Other Life-Principles," pp. 23-24.

3. See the Section, "The BT in Relation to Fertilization and Variation," pp. 36-38.

NEEDS, DRIVES AND THE BT [1]

In the preceding Section, "Instinct and the BT," it was stated that what distinguishes one form of "instinctual" behavior from another is not the presence of a different psychical dynamism or propelling force of some kind but simply a difference in the form of the behavior itself and, further, that each form of instinctual behavior is a manifestation, in a different context, of the operation of the BT. This statement also has applicability to forms of behavior which may be said to be activated by different types of "needs" or "drives". In other words, *here too, I would say, there are no psychical dynamisms or propelling forces at work — there are merely the various distinguishable forms of behavior themselves and each of these forms of behavior is a manifestation, in a different context, of the operation of the BT.*

In recent years the concept of "needs" or "drives" as psychical dynamisms or propelling forces of some kind has been giving way to an *operational* approach, one defining different types of "needs" or "drives" in terms of *observable* differences, for example, in terms of the relationship between distinguishable conditions of deprivation and distinguishable patterns of behavior. This approach to the definition of "needs" and "drives" has the distinct advantage of circumventing an extremely dubious hypothesis in metaphysics but unfortunately is not without some significant disadvantages of its own. For one thing, it is likely to result in our using need or drive terms in very odd ways. More important, however, is the fact that since it ignores the role of *intermediate* processes, it is likely to yield only *rough correlations* between one factor (e.g., deprivation) and another (e.g., behavior), *not uniform relationships.*

Regardless of whether we proceed operationally or otherwise, however, any attempt to differentiate one type of "need" or "drive" from another confronts this fundamental obstacle, *namely, that the observable (intra-organismic and extra-organismic) facts themselves provide us with no objective basis for employing one classification rather than another. In other words, the classification of "needs" or "drives", like the classification of "instincts," must to a considerable extent be arbitrary and artificial.*

For these reasons, and because the use of separate need or drive *names* is apt to be misleading, falsely suggesting the existence of operants which are sharply separable, I myself do not speak of any *special* "needs" or "drives" whatever. Thus I do not speak of an *aggressive* need or drive or of a *sexual* need or drive or of an *exploratory* need or drive or of a *status-seeking* need or drive or of any *other* such need or drive. Neither, as I have indicated, do I refer to any special "instincts."

How, then, are the facts in regard to behavior to be described? Although this has already been suggested,[2] let me make reference here, by way of clarification, to a few representative situations.

Suppose a sexually normal and susceptible human male perceives an attractive human female. I would say that he tends to approach the female, not in virtue of any sexual or mating "instinct" or "need" or "drive," but simply in virtue of the fact that, in accordance with the BT, he tends to maximize stimulation which is vitalizing.

Or consider what occurs when a human being has what might be called a "need" or "drive" for food. If my body is in a certain state which can be loosely described as a state of hunger and if I see or smell some food (a stimulus object eliciting stimulation), the food elicited stimulation, since it is likely to be vitalizing, will probably, in accordance with the BT, lead me to maximize it, say, by moving towards the food and eating it. The precise way (that is, the exact form or manner) in which *I* maximize the food elicited stimulation will differ somewhat, of course, from the precise way in which *someone else* maximizes such food elicited stimulation, but the maximizing behavior of each of us will conform with the BT.

The same schema applies to what occurs when a *plant* might be said to have a "need" or "drive" for food (e.g., for water, for sunlight, etc.). If a plant is in a certain state which can be loosely described as a state of less-than-optimum food supply, the stimulation it receives from the impinging food (a stimulus object eliciting stimulation), since it is likely to be vitalizing, will probably, in accordance with the BT, lead the plant to maximize it, say, by absorbing the food. Presumably in this case, however, in contrast to the human one just mentioned, the organism does not *feel* any hunger – that is, there is no related stimulation indicator – and presumably too its maximizing response is not one which is subject to conditioning or learning.

Although, as I have indicated, I do not speak of any *special* instincts or needs or drives, I do on occasion, for purely expository purposes, speak of one *general* need or drive, viz., the need or drive for *vitalization,* that is, the need or drive on the part of an organism to respond in accordance with the BT. It should be remembered, however, that when I do so, I am speaking *merely of the Basic Tendency itself.* I am not asserting the existence of any kind of entity whose existence is not already implied in my statement of the BT. Certainly I am not asserting the existence of any kind of extra-scientific entity, e.g., an "elan vital" or a "will to live." [3]

1. What is said in this Section in regard to needs and drives also applies, at least in considerable degree, to motives.

2. See the Section, "The Basic Tendency," pp. 5-6 and pp. 10-12.

3. As I have stated elsewhere, a living organism consists only of its physical components and, where it is a percipient or sentient organism, of certain stimulation indicators as well.

THE TERRITORIAL IMPERATIVE [1]

I regard the notion of a "territorial imperative," more specifically, the idea that (at least) some species of animals have an instinctual sense of trespass in virtue of which they will aggressively attack certain other animals when and only when they enter "their" territory, as a misinterpretation of the observed facts.

In the first place, the territorial point at which an intruding animal will be attacked, instead of being fixed, as several writers have emphasized, is actually quite variable, as indeed we might expect. Thus an intruder belonging to species A (e.g., homo sapiens) may precipitate attack at a very different (greater or lesser) distance than an intruder belonging to species B (e.g., a squirrel or a worm) and individual differences between members of the intruding species (e.g., in their size or coloring or odor or degree of familiarity), and differences in the circumstances of the intrusion, may also alter the timing of the retaliatory response.[2] Moreover, under certain conditions, an animal, far from standing its ground and aggressively attacking the intruder, will seek to escape from it, or will resort to some other non-aggressive response such as "playing dead." For under certain conditions such a response will elicit stimulation which is less devitalizing (more vitalizing).[3] These facts would seem to me to suggest (1) that if any "territorial imperative" exists, its operative dimensions are at least highly variable and (2) that an animal's preservation of "its territory" may be less "imperative" – in terms of the BT, less vitalizing – than its preservation of itself.

In support of the existence of a "territorial imperative," some writers have pointed to the reduced aggressivity of an animal when it is on "foreign" territory. But is it necessary or even useful to assume that this change in behavior occurs because the "territorial imperative" then ceases to be activated? When an animal is in a relatively unfamiliar environment, it presumably has a greater need (tendency) to be cautious since as yet it has had an insufficient opportunity to "test out," so to speak, the possible sources of danger. I would suggest that it manifests less aggressiveness toward an intruder under *such* circumstances, *not* because of the cessation of its "territorial imperative," but in part at least because the cautiousness or fearfulness – or, rather, that aspect of the stimulus situation which gives rise to this cautiousness or fearfulness – inhibits or conflicts with its aggressiveness, that is, in some degree activates a withdrawing rather than an attacking response. And conversely I would suggest that it manifests *greater* aggressiveness toward an intruder in a relatively *familiar* environment, *not* because of the *operation* of its "territorial imperative," but in part at least because of the relative *absence* under such circumstances of such a counteracting factor in the stimulus situation. Moreover, and this is a no less important consideration, when an animal is in a relatively familiar environment, any intrusion by an unfamiliar animal, even an unfamiliar *object*, indeed any significant environmental alteration of any kind, serves in some degree to disrupt that familiarity and with it the animal's accumulated sense of safety, perhaps even its sense of wholeness or identity.[4] In less subjective terms, it is devitalized.

1. Since "the territorial imperative" is conceived to be "instinctual", this Section should be read in connection with the Section, "Instinct and the BT", pp. 39-41.

2. As animal A moves closer to animal B, it is likely (other things being equal) to elicit stronger and stronger stimulation within B. Unless, therefore, the V and DV stimulation is such as to result in conflict or is so overwhelming as to be paralyzing (see the Section, "The Genesis of Psychopathology," pp. 160-165), the probability that B will make some

overt response to A progressively increases. Which of the possible overt responses it does make will be determined by, or rather will be in accordance with, the BT.

3. In this case, since even the "thought" (anticipation) of the devitalization which *would* result from standing its ground or from attacking is *itself* somewhat devitalizing, the organism turns away from the intruder, i.e., minimizes the stimulation it induces.

4. See the Section, "Animism, Psychopathology and Devitalization", p. 135.

THE EVOLUTIONARY EMERGENCE OF STIMULATION INDICATORS

If the biological scientist is correct – and I do not wish to doubt that he is – it was only after the evolutionary process eventuated in the emergence of relatively advanced forms of life that the first rudimentary sensory experiences occurred[1] or, in my terminology, the first stimulation indicators.

I see the occurrence of the first stimulation indicator as an event which, in the history of life on this planet, was second in importance only to the beginning of life itself. For one thing, it *marked the emergence of a physical device – a kind of stimulus transforming and magnifying device – which was significantly to increase the adaptive capacity of organisms* and hence greatly to accelerate the future course of the evolutionary process itself. For another thing, its own emergence, as a consequence of that device, *marked the appearance of what, from the ontological or metaphysical point of view, was an entirely new type of entity, namely, a "non-physical" or "psychical" entity, that is to say, an entity not located in physical, or as I prefer to say public, space-time.*[2]

It seems likely that the first sensory experiences were limited to registering the fact, fuzzily and uncertainly, that something or other was happening, that a change of some sort was occurring. With the passage of time, however, stimulation indicators must have become more determinate and hence more informative, yielding rudimentary impressions of particular entities, the first "impressions" perhaps being literally (i.e., physically) just that.

Along with the evolutionary refinement of the sensory

apparatus, there was, of course, a comparable development of the cognitive apparatus. Thus there was a beginning, then an increasing, capacity to "remember," to "expect," to "judge," etc. The emergence of images in connection with such responses represented not only a further development of sensory indicators but also their partial replacement. For the ability to "imagine" the consequences of some possible action enables us to set our course without having to experience its consequences on a sensory level.

Does the cognitive apparatus of Man involve, either directly or indirectly, the presence of any *third* type of ontological entity? I would say not, that even the most complex psychological responses entail nothing more than the occurrence of certain physical processes and the possible presence of certain stimulation indicators.[3]

1. Sentience is a characteristic which presumably is not possessed by any earth-rooted species, no matter how complex or "advanced" their structure. Perhaps their evolutionary *need* for sentience has been less compelling since, in view of their relative immobility, they normally come in contact with a narrower range of stimulus situations.

2. See the Section, "Metaphysical Dualism," pp. 56-61.

3. See the Section, "Psychical Entities," pp. 95-100.

PART THREE

THE WORLD OF PHILOSOPHY

EPISTEMOLOGICAL MONISM VERSUS EPISTEMOLOGICAL DUALISM

For more than 2000 years, philosophers have been concerned with the question: What is the content or object or datum of such psychological processes as perception, cognition, memory, etc.? Is it something "objective" or something "subjective"? Is it the external object or situation itself or is it something which intervenes (mediates) between the external object or situation and the organism? In recent years, psychologists also have been concerned with this question – I should say, with these questions – though for the most part they have been ready to accept one or the other of the answers which have been provided by philosophy or by physical science.

Let us look for a moment at a question which is being debated in academic psychological circles today. An examination of *this* question will, I suggest, prepare the way for an answer to our *philosophical* question.

In current expositions of learning theory, we find seemingly conflicting statements not only concerning the *mechanics* of learning but also concerning the *content* of learning, in regard to *what* it is that is learned. Some writers have asserted that what is learned is always a connection between a stimulus and a response. On the other hand, other writers have maintained that an organism can learn a connection (sequence) between one stimulus and another stimulus, can "learn the environment", as it has been phrased.[1] These contentions would certainly *appear* to be quite incompatible but of course they *are* incompatible only so far as they represent mutually exclusive views as to what it is that actually occurs in learning.

Now I suspect that the first group of writers would not deny that when learning occurs, it is *as if* one stimulus gets connected with another. And I suspect that the second group would not deny that when learning occurs, it is *as if* a stimulus gets connected with a response. Thus I would suggest that their apparent disagreement is related to the fact that the first group has chosen to use the term "learning" in such a way that the object of learning is always a stimulus-response connection and the second group has chosen to use the term "learning" in such a way that the object of learning may be a stimulus-stimulus sequence. I would not wish to contend that there are no differences of opinion between the groups in regard to the *facts themselves*, but merely that there is at least this *terminological* difference.

I think we can deal in a comparable way with our historic philosophical question. In other words, we must distinguish between the *factual question as to what actually occurs* when we are said to be perceiving something or remembering something or thinking about something, etc., and the *terminological question as to what is to be designated* as the "content" or "object" or "datum" or "referend," etc. of such acts or processes. I believe that much of the disagreement concerning the answer to our philosophical question is traceable to the failure to make this simple but important distinction.

As for the facts themselves, it seems clear that when we are engaged in perceiving, remembering, judging, thinking, etc., there are certain physical (including neurological) processes which are occurring and possibly certain stimulation indicators as well. Suppose, for example, I can be correctly described as looking at or seeing a tree. In this case the light waves reflected by the tree are impinging upon the retina of my eye and initiating certain impulses which, as these reach my brain, give rise to the "sight" (i.e., a stimulation indicator) of that tree. These are the facts. But am I in this hypothetical case of veridical perception seeing the stimulus object (or a part of the object) *itself* or some *subjective visual representation* of that object (or of a part of that object)? How we answer *this* question, I would say, *is merely a matter of terminological choice.* Doubtless it is more in accord with everyday usage to make the "what" of veridical perception, as well as the "what" of certain other veridical psychological responses, the external object or situation itself. But this usage should not mislead us, of course, as to the facts themselves, in particular, should not deceive us into believing that we have any more – or any less – "direct contact" with any external object or situation than we actually do.

1. I have in mind here, for example, R. S. Woodward's disagreement with the position of C. L. Hull. In stating the disagreement, I have followed *his* (Woodward's) use of the term "stimulus" and "response" rather than my own.

METAPHYSICAL DUALISM

A number of years ago in my doctoral dissertation, *A Critical Examination of the Epistemological and Psychophysical Doctrines of Bertrand Russell* (William Wilkins, Baltimore, 1931), I indicated that I was a metaphysical dualist. For better or for worse, I am still a metaphysical dualist today. That is to say, I find in the world two very basically different kinds of entities, entities some of which I would call "physical" and some of which I would call "non-physical" or "psychical," terms which I use interchangeably.

Of course, given a number of entities, one may classify them in accordance with any characteristic or property one may choose. Thus, given a half dozen entities, one may classify them in such a way that they are of one kind, of two kinds, or of three or more kinds. Similarly one may categorize the entities which comprise the universe in such a way that they are of one kind, of two kinds, or of three or more kinds. Whether one is a "monist" or a "dualist" or a "pluralist," therefore, depends in part upon the dividing principle one decides to employ.

Related to this point is another, no less obvious. Two views of the universe may both be "dualistic", that is, may divide its constituent entities into two kinds but the lines of division may not at all coincide. Thus one may have a dichotomy between the organic and the inorganic, or between the human and the non-human, or between the visible and the invisible, etc. In brief, there may be a multiplicity of "dualisms."

I have said above that I find in the world "two very basically different kinds of entities." What do I mean by "basically different"? Isn't the difference between the inorganic and the organic, for example, a "basic" difference? Or the difference between entities which *do* exist and those which *did* exist or *will* exist? It is not easy to spell out exactly what I *do* mean by a "basic" difference, but let me try.

By a "basic" difference between two entities, I mean one in virtue of which the entities have a different kind of *ontological* status, that is, a different kind of status with respect to the level or form (the defining conditions) of their *existence*. Furthermore I would say that the fewer properties two such ontologically different entities have in common, the *more* basic the difference between them is.[1]

Now if I look around, so to speak, at the world in which I live, it seems to me that the *most* basic difference is between those entities which I would call "physical" and those entities which I would call "non-physical" or "psychical."[2] Within the physical category I would include, and include only, the "ultimate" units of matter and energy and the various groupings and combinations of them which make up what has been called the material universe, not excluding, of course, those combinations which form the bodies of living organisms.[3] Within the psychical category I would include, and include only, stimulation indicators, that is, (the subjective components of) sights, sounds, odors, tastes, tactile sensations, other bodily sensations and images.

Of course the occurrence of a stimulation indicator — e.g., the occurrence of the sound I hear when I press down on a key of my piano — is causally related to an antecedent *physical* process, specifically, to the sound waves which impinge upon the cochlea of my ear and to the impulses which are then transmitted to my brain. *But the sound itself* (usually I refer to this as the "subjective component" of the sound, etc.) *is not the same as, is not identical with, the sound waves or the impulses or any other physical event or process which may occur within my brain.* It is, in fact, a "very basically different kind of entity", that is, it has a very different kind of status with respect to the level or form (the defining conditions) of its existence.

Thus the sound does not have a position in space, that is, in the same space as does a *physical* entity (e.g., my body). Indeed, the statement that a particular *sound* (as distinct from the *source* of the sound) is a certain distance in space from me impresses one immediately as being a somewhat "odd" statement and of a very different kind from the statement, e.g., that the *piano* is a certain distance from me. In the latter case, the distance between the terms of the relationship – that is, the piano and my body – can be determined by using one and the same operational procedure, e.g., by extending a tape measure between them. In the former case, there is *no* uniform means of measurement which can be applied.

If we talk about a "sight" instead of a sound, these remarks are equally applicable. Consider, e.g., the sight I see when I look at a distant star. That sight, to be sure, *appears* to be located at a certain point or region in "outer" space. But here too there is no uniform procedure by which we can compute the distance between that sight and, let us say, my body, for the two *terms* of the relationship are too different to lend themselves to a single method of measurement. What we *can* measure is the distance between one physical entity (or what is presumably the point or region in space it occupies) and another physical entity (or what is presumably the point or region in space *it* occupies). Thus we can measure the distance between my body and the point or region where the sight *appears* to be, or between my body and the external *source* of that sight, but we cannot measure the distance between my body and the *sight itself*.

This point can be made clearer, perhaps, by the following statements. If the sight I see when I look at a distant star is generated in the manner indicated but is "out there" in space, this implies that I have the capacity to project something into a point or region of space millions of light years away, and that I can do this within the proverbial "twinkling of an eye." And presumably other percipient organisms have a similar capacity. The absurdity of such a supposition makes it evident that stimulation indicators, in contrast to physical entities, are *not* located in public space.[4] And for similar reasons, we can conclude that stimulation indicators, in contrast to physical entities, are *not* located in public *time* or, if one prefers, in public space-time. (Since stimulation indicators obviously occur and are perceived as having spatio-temporal relationships of their *own*,[5] I speak of them as being present in "private" space-time.)

A second difference between stimulation indicators and physical entities is this, that the former have *ontological dependence*, the latter, *ontological independence*. That is to say, whereas the existence of a stimulation indicator always presupposes (i.e., is conditional upon) the presence of some physical entity, the existence of a physical entity does *not* always presuppose – indeed, I would say, *never* presupposes – the existence of some stimulation indicator. Thus stimulation indicators can occur only when some kind of neurophysiological perceiving apparatus, some kind of nervous system, has been appropriately stimulated. But various types of physical entities can occur (and certainly did occur for millions of years prior to the development of any percipient organisms on this earth) without the presence of any stimulation indicators.

A third differentiating factor relates to the *epistemological* status of physical entities and of stimulation indicators. I have indicated in the preceding Section that whether we designate as the "what" of veridical perception, memory, etc. the stimulation indicator or (some segment of) the entity itself is a *terminological* matter, at least once we have agreed as to what actually *occurs*. It is nonetheless a fact, however, that when I can be correctly described as perceiving (or remembering or thinking about, etc.) some physical entity – say, my piano – the *stimulation indicator* which may be present has a different epistemological relationship to me than does the *piano itself*. Thus the *stimulation indicator* which is, in some sense, perceived by me *cannot* be perceived, in that sense, by any *other* percipient organism. On the other hand, the *physical entity* – in this case, the piano – which is, in some sense, perceived by me *can* be perceived, in that sense, by another percipient organism. To state the matter differently. Nobody else can experience my "sights" any more than he can experience my feelings. But our different sights can be activated by the same stimulus object. The former, I will say, are "subjective," the latter, "objective."

To summarize: stimulation indicators, in contrast to physical entities, (1) do not have location in public space-time, (2) have ontological dependence and (3) are subjective. In my terminology, stimulation indicators are "non-physical," i.e., "psychical."[6]

1. This qualification makes the differences between past, present and future entities *less* basic.

2. A competitor for the honor might be thought to be the difference, which has long been a subject of philosophical controversy, between "particulars" and "universals". But I am speaking here only of entities which have *existence* (*reality*), that is, of entities which are present in public space-time or in some private space-time. (In regard to private space-time, see elsewhere in this Section. Also see the Section, "The Definition of Existence and Reality," pp. 74-77.)

3. According to modern physics, a physical object — e.g., my desk — is composed ultimately of a variety of innumerable, and theoretically unobservable, particles or "wavicles". I find no difficulty, as some philosophers apparently do, in asserting that *both* the collection *and* its constituent particles or "wavicles" *exist;* or in admitting that the collection elicits a sensory impression of object solidarity which is very different from the largely-empty-space nature of the object itself.

4. If one takes the position that sounds, sights, etc. are located in one's own head, this absurdity is avoided. But the neurophysiological evidence does not support such a view! There is no evidence, e.g., that when one hears something or touches something or smells something, a little sound

or a little touch or a little odor is inside one's skull, is literally a part of one's head! It seems equally absurd to maintain that the sound or touch or odor, little or big, instead of being activated by the interrelationship between the stimulus object and the organism, is literally a part of the stimulus object itself. The legs of my piano are literally a part of the piano but the sounds made by my piano are certainly not!

5. Thus I may meaningfully say of a stimulation indicator of mine (e.g., a flash of lightning) that it had a certain spatial relationship to (e.g., was to the right of) some other stimulation indicator of mine (e.g., a dark mass of gray indicating a cloud) or that it had a certain temporal relationship to (e.g., occurred to me before) some other stimulation indicator of mine (e.g., a clap of thunder). To say that stimulation indicators are present in "private" space-time is merely an abbreviated way of summarizing such facts. See the Section, "The Definition of Existence and Reality," pp. 74-77.

6. It is not being asserted, of course, that the three differentiating properties mentioned are the *only* differentiating properties. Implicit in, or otherwise related to, these differences are various *secondary* differences. Of the three differentiating properties specified, the *essential* or *defining* property of an entity which is "non-physical" or "psychical", as I use these terms, is that it is *not in public space-time*. See the Section, "The Basic Tendency," p. 7, or "The Evolutionary Emergence of Stimulation Indicators", p. 48.

PSYCHOPHYSICAL INTERACTIONISM

It is the accepted scientific view — and I do not wish to question this — that when (the subjective component of) a particular sight, sound, odor, taste, tactile sensation, etc. — what I call a "stimulation indicator" — occurs, there was some antecedent neurological event which in some sense "brought it about" or "caused it." Indeed it seems to be held that in such a situation some neurological occurrence O_1 is so related to that subsequent occurrence O_2 that normally O_1 will not occur without being followed by O_2 and O_2 will not occur without having been preceded by O_1.[1] Now if there *is* an O_1 which is so related to O_2 (that is, to a stimulation indicator), and if "bringing about" or "causing" an occurrence is equated with having such a one-to-one relationship to that occurrence, we can draw this significant conclusion with respect to some subsequent occurrence O_3 — e.g., some further neurological event or some overt response of that organism — namely, that if O_1 has brought about (caused) O_3, so has O_2, and that if O_2 has brought about (caused) O_3, so has O_1.[2] In other words, we cannot maintain that the *neurological event* O_1 *has* brought about (caused) O_3 and that the *indicator* O_2 *has not;* and we cannot maintain that the *indicator* O_2 *has* brought about (caused) O_3 and that the *neurological event* O_1 *has not.*

This conclusion, though clearly implicit in our premises, is one which apparently has often been overlooked. Yet it has a direct bearing upon the age-old question of psychophysical interaction, sometimes referred to as "the mind-body" problem. For if, as maintained in the preceding Section, an indicator is non-physical, i.e., psychical, and a neurological event is physical, then, on the premises stated and on the seemingly valid additional assumption that there *is* some subsequent physical occurrence (for example, a neurological event or an overt response) to which *either* O_1 *or* O_2 has such a one-to-one relationship, it follows (1) that something physical brings about or causes something psychical, (2) that something psychical brings about or causes something physical and (3) that something physical brings about or causes something physical.[3] If statements 1 and 2 are true, in other words, if there is a two-way causal relationship between the physical and the psychical, then there is *psychophysical interaction.*

Of course, if we were to make *different* terminological or factual assumptions, we might arrive at some *other* conclusion. Thus if being "brought about" or "caused" by something were equated, as it very frequently is, with (what in the preceding Section I have called) being "ontologically dependent" upon that something, a concept which entails something more than a mere one-to-one sequential relationship, we might arrive at the conclusion that whereas the physical brings about or causes the psychical, the psychical does *not* bring about or cause the physical.[4]

Doubtless the "moral" of all this is the not-very-surprising one that to look upon any statement or descriptive label of a philosophical (or other) position without giving due regard to its terminological and factual suppositions can be grossly misleading.

1. In referring to the re-occurrence of an event, I am referring, of course, to the re-occurrence not of the *numerically* identical event (which is an impossibility) but of a *qualitatively* identical event.

2. It might be helpful to concretize the matter by using as an example the knee jerk or patellar reflex, letting O_1 designate a certain neurological event, O_2 the sensation of having the knee struck and O_3 either a certain subsequent neurological event or the movement of the leg itself. O_4, mentioned later, might designate the sensation experienced in connection with the leg movement.

3. If we assume that there is a subsequent psychical occurrence (i.e., a subsequent stimulation indicator) — let us designate this O_4 — to which O_2

has such a one-to-one relationship, then it also follows that something psychical brings about or causes something psychical. In the example cited, O_4 might be the kinesthetic sensation experienced in connection with the overt response O_3.

4. Our psychophysical conclusions will *also* vary, of course, with different concepts of the "physical" and different concepts of the "psychical".

DETERMINISM VERSUS INDETERMINISM

With respect to at least a great many of the actions which we and others perform, it is quite common to hold that some *alternative* action *might* have been performed *instead.* Thus it may be maintained that though we told him this, we *might* have told him that; or that though someone did this, he *might* have done that; and so on. Nor do we confine this kind of statement to the actions of human beings, or to the actions of other living organisms. Thus we may say that though the lightning struck one place, it *might* have struck some other place, or that though a tire blew out at one time, it *might* have blown out at some other time; and so on.

The question I wish to raise here is this: In order for statements of this sort to be true, must scientific determinism be false? In other words, does the truth of statements of this sort presuppose a position which is *incompatible* with scientific determinism? On the surface, it would certainly *seem* that the two positions *are* incompatible. For the statements appear to presuppose that from one and the same set of antecedent conditions, *either one* of the two alternative consequences could follow. But though the statements in question *can* so be interpreted, they *can* be interpreted as implying something much more modest than this. Thus they can be interpreted as implying *merely* that what occurs, as well as the hypothetical alternative (mutually exclusive) event which does not occur, are both consistent causally with what little is *known* of the antecedent conditions, with no implication being made as to whether or not both of the events actually *are* consistent causally with those antecedent conditions. In other words, the statements *may* be presupposing merely an "epistemological" indeterminism.

But what of the merits of scientific (or, as I would say, ontological) determinism itself? Let us define scientific or ontological *indeterminism* as the hypothesis that at least sometimes when one state of affairs differs qualitatively (not merely numerically) from another state of affairs, their antecedent conditions are in every respect qualitatively the same (i.e., exactly alike). And let us define scientific or ontological *determinism* as the denial of this, that is, as the hypothesis that whenever one state of affairs differs qualitatively from another state of affairs, their antecedent conditions are at least in some respect qualitatively different. *In my judgment, the indeterministic hypothesis is self-contradictory and the deterministic hypothesis is tautological.*

Let us try to suppose that, in accordance with the indeterminist's hypothesis, we *do* have two different (i.e., qualitatively different) states of affairs whose antecedent conditions are in every respect qualitatively the same (i.e., exactly alike). (To concretize the matter, suppose that one state of affairs is my decision to turn to the right and the other state of affairs is my decision to turn to the left, or that one state of affairs is the movement of an electron at a given velocity and direction and the other state of affairs is the movement of that electron at a different velocity or direction.) But if there are, per hypothesis, two qualitatively different states of affairs, *can* their antecedent conditions really be in every respect qualitatively exactly alike? Don't the antecedent conditions in the *one* instance, being something more than *merely* antecedent, have the characteristic of evoking (or eliciting or inducing or giving rise to, etc.) *one* state of affairs and the antecedent conditions in the *other* instance, being something more than *merely* antecedent, have the characteristic of evoking (or eliciting or inducing or giving rise to, etc.) the *other* (*qualitatively different*) state of affairs? And if something – in this case a set of conditions – has *different* characteristics in the two instances, how can it be qualitatively exactly alike in the two instances?

Characteristics are, of course, of different kinds and where a characteristic is "relational" rather than "intrinsic," it would commonly be said that something *can* be qualitatively exactly alike in two instances even though *such* a characteristic changes — for example, that the same unchanged object can be in one place at one time and in some other place at some other time. But it seems very clear that the characteristic of evoking (or eliciting or inducing or giving rise to, etc.) a certain state of affairs must be construed as an "intrinsic," not as a "relational," characteristic — that it must be construed as entailing something about the *constituent nature* of that which it characterizes. Hence if a set of antecedent conditions has *one* such characteristic in *one* instance and some *other* such characteristic in some *other* instance, it *cannot* be qualitatively exactly alike in the two instances. *It follows, therefore, that the indeterminist's hypothesis is self-contradictory and that the determinist's hypothesis, which is a denial of the indeterminist's hypothesis, is a tautology.*[1]

If the indeterministic hypothesis, as defined above, were correct — in other words, if at least sometimes the antecedent conditions of two qualitatively different states of affairs were in every respect qualitatively the same (i.e., exactly alike) — it would follow that, even if we had a complete knowledge of those conditions, at least *some* states of affairs would be theoretically unpredictable. For A might evoke B in one instance and C in some other instance. In virtue of this consequence, it is not surprising that the deterministic-indeterministic conflict should frequently be stated in terms of theoretical predictability or in terms of the related concept of universal law. I would like to point out, however, that *the concept of theoretical predictability is a derivative or secondary concept* and that the definition of the deterministic-indeterministic controversy which I have presented in this Section is both *more basic and less ambiguous.*

In this connection, let me make brief reference to Heisenberg's so-called "Principle of Indeterminacy." This principle states, in effect, as is well known, that there are certain observational limits which we encounter in the investigation of sub-atomic particles which it is not even *theoretically* possible to transcend. Implicit in this principle is the conclusion that the scientist not only *will not* but *cannot* acquire the knowledge which would be needed in order for him to be able to predict completely the course of future events — as Laplace, for example, envisioned. I would like to point out, however, that the Principle of Indeterminacy is in no respect inconsistent with the deterministic position as I have stated it or even with the derivative thesis that *if* we had a complete knowledge of the past, the future would be theoretically predictable. For the principle merely is a denial of the supposition that we *can* have this complete knowledge.

Since ontological determinism, as here defined, is a tautology, it is applicable no less to the world of animate entities than to the world of inanimate entities. *What basically differentiates the behavior of the former from the behavior of the latter, I would say, is not the operation of ontological indeterminism but rather the operation of the Basic Tendency. Whether an entity is animate or inanimate, its behavior is ontologically determined but only if it is animate do we find it responding in conformity with the BT.*

1. If perchance it should be foolishly asserted that two qualitatively different states of affairs can be *caused* by sets of antecedent conditions which are qualitatively the same (i.e., exactly alike), where the idea of cause entails a one-to-one relationship, it is obvious that an *additional* self-contradiction is involved.

FREE WILL AND FREE CHOICE

In the light of what has been said in the preceding Section, it follows that *so far as any doctrine of free will or free choice presupposes the occurrence of scientific or ontological indeterminism (as such indeterminism is there defined), that doctrine is false — indeed, entails a self-contradiction.* Since undoubtedly there are a great many persons, not excluding some who have given special attention to the matter, who "believe in" the occurrence of this type of free will or free choice, it also follows that a great many persons are *in error* in that belief.[1]

It does *not* follow, of course, that "free will" or "free choice", when construed in some *other* sense, does not occur. Of course today, in contrast to a few generations ago, philosophic discourse contains relatively few references to a "will," either free or determined, since the term is associated with a conception of the mind, as a reservoir of distinct "mental faculties", which no longer has a wide acceptance. Thus in more recent years the problem of "free will" has become increasingly the problem of "free choice."

That there *is* the capacity for "free choice" in one very important sense of that term seems to me evident. Certainly it is meaningful to assert that choosing does occur (though it is difficult to specify exactly what this involves) *and that it makes a difference.* Thus it seems clear that when a person chooses to do X rather than Y (assuming that doing X and doing Y are within his repertoire of responses) he is likely to act *differently* from the way he *would* have acted had he chosen to do Y rather than X. But this fact is in no way inconsistent with the view that a difference in choice is always related to some difference in the antecedent conditions. In other words, free choice in *this* sense is in no way inconsistent with the *deterministic* position set forth in the preceding Section.[2]

1. It is frequently asserted that if Man's behavior is "determined", he cannot be "responsible" for any of his actions. But the validity of this inference depends, of course, on just how these terms are being used. If, e.g., "determined" is employed in the sense I have specified and if "responsibility" occurs where behavior may be correctly described as being "deliberate" or "planned", *no* incompatibility need be present.

2. The capacity for "free will" or "free choice" has traditionally been claimed exclusively, or at least primarily, for members of homo sapiens. However, it is only by resorting to some quite dubious factual assumptions (and/or by defining these terms quite arbitrarily) that any differentiation in this respect can be sustained.

ACTION AND RECIPROCAL INTERACTION

If A is "acting upon" or "affecting" B, B *may or may not*, in the same sense, be "acting upon" or "affecting" A. For although there are *some* senses in which "acting upon" or "affecting" *is* a symmetrical relationship, there are *other* senses in which "acting upon" or "affecting" *is not* a symmetrical relationship.

If "acting upon" or "affecting" is equated, e.g., with "coming into physical contact with," the relationship *is* a symmetrical one; for if in *this* sense A is "acting upon" or "affecting" B, B *must* be "acting upon" or "affecting" A. On the other hand, if "acting upon" or "affecting" is equated, e.g., with "bringing about a change in," the relationship *is not* a symmetrical one; for if in *this* sense A is "acting upon" or "affecting" B, B *need not* be "acting upon" or "affecting" A. To illustrate the latter statement: if certain sun spots are "affecting" the operation of my radio, the operation of my radio need not be "affecting" the sun spots.

This distinction is relevant to a philosophical puzzle which may be posed as follows: "In order for A to act upon or affect B, it would certainly seem as if A and B would have to be present at the same time. But if acting upon or affecting is always a relationship between two things which are present at the same time, how can the past ever affect the present or the present affect the future?" The answer is that "acting upon" and "affecting" entail simultaneity *only* where we are using these words in a *symmetrical* sense; they do *not* entail simultaneity where, as in this puzzle, we are using them in an *asymmetrical* sense.

CAUSATION

If we are able correctly to say of a certain set of (one or more) conditions that each of these conditions is *necessary* for the occurrence of some event E and that together they are *sufficient* for the occurrence of the event E, few scientists would hesitate to call that set of conditions C the "cause" of E. Of course, the term "cause" is very frequently used – in science and elsewhere – in other, usually less exacting or "looser," senses. Indeed we may designate something as the "cause" of some event E when admittedly it is *neither* necessary *nor* sufficient for the occurrence of E, as when we say that heavy drinking is the cause of many automobile accidents or that inadequate birth control information is the cause of overpopulation or that deep depression is the cause of suicide.[1]

If, in the sense I have indicated, some set of conditions C *is* the "cause" of an event E, then C and E must have a one-to-one relationship to one another, that is, neither will occur (regardless of how we may vary the circumstances) without the other. For if C were to occur without E, C would not be *sufficient* for the occurrence of E and if E were to occur without C, C would not be *necessary* for the occurrence of E. Generally speaking, it is much more difficult to ascertain what is *necessary* for the occurrence of E than it is to ascertain what is *sufficient* for the occurrence of E.[2]

If C will not occur (regardless of the circumstances which may in fact intervene) without E and E will not occur (regardless of the circumstances which may in fact intervene) without C, there is an *unvarying* relationship between the two but not ipso facto an *invariable* relationship, that is, an invariant relationship which is *logically necessary*. The relationship between C and E will approach *invariability* only as C and E approach identity; and as this becomes so the so-called causal relationship actually becomes one of entailment. Thus we may say that *ultimately causation is not an empirical relationship between non-identical terms but a logical relationship between identical terms and hence that the ultimate laws of empirical science are reducible to the basic laws (i.e., tautologies) of logic.*

1. For the physicist causation involves correlated transformations within two matter-energy systems. But since causation is a *relationship*, the problem of defining cause is essentially the same regardless of the *terms* of that relationship.

2. It is sometimes supposed, particularly in the area of mechanics, that a "cause" somehow *compels* the occurrence of its "effect". But to presume that there exists some kind of a "compelling force" over and above the terms of the causal relationship itself is, I believe, to move from the world of fact to the world of animistic fantasy.

THE DEFINITION OF EXISTENCE AND REALITY

Philosophers who have sought to define such concepts or terms[1] as existence or reality have, in general, considered the task to be a logically feasible one. But some — for example, Alvin Thalheimer in *Existential Metaphysics*[2] — have held otherwise, contending that where a basic *ontological* concept or term is involved, we are necessarily presupposing in our definition just what we are seeking to define. In other words, we are "begging the question." For in asserting that to have reality or existence or being or actuality, etc. is to have some property X (for example, to have a locus within public space and time), we are asserting, it is argued, that to have reality or existence or being, etc. is *really* or *actually* or *in fact* to have the property X — that is to say, to have it in the *real* or *actual* world — in contrast to merely *seeming* or *being imagined* to have the property X.

This criticism is, it seems to me, essentially sound, though I would feel some need to make the following comments by way of clarification.

(1) When we are setting forth a definition, be it of an ontological or non-ontological term, we are not *necessarily* making this *particular kind* of assertion. For example, we may be saying *merely* that in such-and-such a context — say, in this article or in this book — we plan to use one verbal symbol interchangeably with a certain other (more complex) verbal symbol. Obviously if this is *all* we are asserting, the alleged circularity need not be present.

(2) Nor is the difficulty in question *confined*, as I see it, to the definition of these *basic ontological* terms (or to their synonyms, their grammatical variations, or their linguistic

equivalents in other languages). For we may also involve ourselves in circularity in defining certain *ontologically related* terms, for example, the term "truth" (or its synonyms, variations or translations) or in defining certain *equational* terms, for example, the term "being identical with" or the term "being equivalent to" (or its synonyms, variations or translations). Thus in defining the "truth" of a statement or proposition, etc., we may be saying in effect that a statement or proposition, etc. is "true" if it *truly* has the property X. And in defining "being identical with" or "being equivalent to", we may be saying in effect that to be "identical" with such-and-such is to be *identical* with such-and-such or to be "equivalent" to such-and-such is to be *equivalent* to such-and-such. The circularity in the latter instances results from the fact that a definition usually is *itself*, explicitly or implicitly, a statement of an identity or of an equivalence of some sort.

(3) Although an assertion to the effect that something exists or is real if it has the property X may be circular (may beg the question), it does not follow that it may not be helpful in facilitating communication. In point of fact, it may be quite useful in this respect, particularly, perhaps, in indicating what one does *not* mean. With this consoling thought in mind, let me turn to, and seek to elaborate upon, my *own* definition of existence and reality.

As I have already had occasion to note,[3] *an entity "exists" or "is real," as I use these terms, if and only if it is present in either public space-time or in some private space-time.* By "public" space-time, I mean, of course, the space-time of the physical sciences, that is, the all-embracing network of spatio-temporal relationships in which are located the entities which make up the material universe. By a "private" space-time, I mean a subjective space-time, that is, a network of spatio-temporal relationships in which an organism's stimulation indicators are located.[4] Thus, within a field of sensory experience, one may perceive one entity (say, a patch of blue) as being in one place, some other entity (say, a patch of green) as being in some other place – say, to the right of it – or one entity (say, a flash of lightning) as being present in one's experience before or after or at the same time as some other entity (say, a clap of thunder). Normally (unless we are hallucinating or are otherwise misperceiving) there is a significant degree of correspondence between the subjective network of spatio-temporal relationships linking the stimulation indicators and the objective network of spatio-temporal relationships linking their external stimulus sources.

Under the definition which I have given, the question may be asked: "Do *relationships* – for example, spatio-temporal relationships – exist or have reality?" The answer, I would say, is that they do not, for *a relationship is not itself present in, in the sense of being an occupant of, public or private space-time; only its terms may be.* To be sure, we may frequently talk *as if* some relationship were in some manner present in space-time. Thus we may say that a certain relationship – for example, the relationship of "being ten feet from" or of "being larger than" – was or has been or will be present between this and that object, or between this and that patch of color, for such-and-such a length of time. But clearly a relationship is not space-time *filling,* that is, is not an *occupant* of space-time, at least not in the same sense in which its *terms* may be occupants. Thus a relationship can be said to "exist" or to be "real," as I have defined these words, only if one is speaking very loosely, only if one is actually referring to the existence or reality of the *terms* of the relationship. Where the terms of a relationship *do* exist (*are* real), I prefer to describe the relationship, therefore, not as "existing" (or as "being real") but simply as "being present."[5]

1. In this Section I have sought to avoid the (terminological) question

as to whether it is words or concepts which are defined. I believe the cogency of the points made here, however, in no way depends on how one may choose to answer this question.

2. Thalheimer, Alvin; *Existential Metaphysics*, Philosophical Library, 1960,

3. See the Section, "Metaphysical Dualism," p. 60.

4. However neither "network of spatio-temporal relationships" is itself an existent. See the following paragraph in this Section.

5. Although throughout this book I have tried to avoid speaking of a relationship as "existing" or as "being real," I do at times say either of a relationship or of an entity which exists or is real that it "is" or "is present" or "takes place" or "occurs," etc. These terms are employed mainly for the sake of verbal variety, although where "taking place" or "occurring" or a similar term is used, my purpose is to give emphasis to the emerging or fleeting, in contrast to the continuing, character of the entity.

MATTER, PROPERTY COMPLEXES AND SCIENTIFIC REALISM

It is customary for the physical scientist to think of a physical entity — whether a macrocosmic entity such as a star or a desk or a microcosmic entity such as an atom or an electron — as a *something* (often as a physical "substance") *which has or possesses certain properties,* say, a certain mass or a certain size or a certain shape. But the question arises: If we should enumerate *all* the properties which this something (or physical substance) has or possesses, what is it that would remain *unenumerated?* A something (physical substance) *without* any properties? This appears to be a logical impossibility and a metaphysical absurdity. Yet it would seem that our thinking has been influenced so strongly by the subject-predicate structure of our language — that is, by our linguistic habit of attributing a property to something — that it is difficult *not* to conceive of a physical entity in this way.[1]

I believe it would help the physical scientist to avoid this predicament if he were to think of a physical entity as consisting of the *properties themselves,* more specifically, as being *an interrelated aggregate of properties, or a property complex, which pervades a certain area of public space-time.* In any case we must remember that the observations made by the physical scientist *can never justify the postulation of a propertyless "it" which has or possesses certain properties but only the postulation of the properties themselves.*

In recent years there has been some tendency on the part of the physical scientist to depart from his traditionally realistic or objectivistic conception of the material world – that is to say, of physical (material) entities – and to accept instead a relativistic or subjectivistic point of view. The impetus for this change appears to have come largely from the Theory of Relativity, on the one hand, and from revised hypotheses concerning atomic structure, on the other. In any case, the result has been an increasingly "abstract" material world which can no longer be "pictured" or "visualized" and which seemingly has all but lost its familiar substantiality and solidity. However, the conclusion which is apparently being drawn by some physical scientists, that the entities which ultimately comprise our physical universe are merely scientific constructs or mathematical fictions rather than realities,[2] is one which I cannot accept.

Characteristic of this position is the assertion that a physical entity is nothing more than a kind of mathematical curve in a four-dimensional space-time continuum, nothing more than a set of mathematical equations. As a "scientific realist," however, I would have to point out that although a physical entity may be (to a greater or lesser degree) *describable in terms of* a set of mathematical equations, it *cannot be identical with* a set of mathematical equations, any more than a stimulation indicator, such as (the subjective component of) a sight or sound, can be identical with the light waves or sound waves which serve to elicit it.[3] For one thing, mathematical *equations* consist of mathematical *symbols* and we can hardly suppose that we ourselves, and the world around us, are, to put it bluntly, a set of marks on a sheet of paper or even the "ideas" these marks may represent!

1. Since I am referring in this Section to *anything* which is physical, including a light wave or a globule of water or a puff of smoke, I use the term "physical entity" rather than the term "physical object," which usually is construed in a narrower sense.

2. See the Section, "The Definition of Existence and Reality," pp. 75-77.

3. See the Section, "Metaphysical Dualism," pp. 57-61.

THE ORDERLINESS IN THE UNIVERSE

We live in a universe in which there is an impressive degree of orderliness, that is to say, in which events and relationships exhibit an impressive degree of patternization.[1] Whether we direct our attention to the movement of the planets around the Sun or to the succession of the Earth's seasons or to the cyclical or rhythmical nature of many aspects of the life process itself, that orderliness is plainly evident. Those with teleological inclinations have long looked upon such phenomena as indicating the operation of some sort of overall purpose or plan and hence as demonstrating the existence (at least at the moment when the universe had its beginning) of some kind of supernatural being or beings.

I should like to point out, however, that whatever the theological possibilities may be, *much of the orderliness in the universe stems from the combined operation of two quite mundane facts. One is that the universe is deterministic.*[2] *The other is that because of the limited operation of disrupting factors, physical entities (at least on some level, either macrocosmic or microcosmic*[3]*) maintain their causally relevant intrinsic properties*[4] *unchanged, or essentially unchanged,*[5] *for a humanly significant length of time.*

Consider, for example, the elliptical path traversed by the Earth in relation to the Sun. Given a deterministic universe, since the "causally relevant intrinsic properties" of the two bodies – more specifically, since their masses – remain "essentially unchanged" during the journey, the Earth's orbit, so far as it is a product of unchanging properties (and thus so far as there are no intruding bodies with significantly interfering properties), could not be anything *other* than a markedly regular one. And the logic of the situation is exactly the same, of course, regardless of the particular causal relationship we may be considering.

I have said that *much* of the orderliness in the universe stems from the two facts specified. Clearly, however, *not all* of the orderliness does – or rather, *not the specific character of the orderliness.* Thus the *specific character* of the markedly regular path pursued by the Earth is a function not merely of determinism and of what, for the sake of brevity, we might call "property persistence" but also of the *specific character* of the persistent properties of (all) the entities involved. It is for *this* reason that the Earth's orbit, markedly regular though it is, is nevertheless quite different from the orbits, markedly regular though they are, of Mercury and Venus and Mars, etc. And a similar comment is applicable to the specific character of any other forms of orderliness or patternization.[6]

1. "Orderliness" (or "patternization"), as here used, is an *objective* relationship, though without the capacity to observe and to differentiate relationships human beings would be unable, of course, to *discern* it. Orderliness (or patternization) may assume a wide variety of different forms. Thus there is orderliness of a sort in the mere fact that 58th Street remains at a fixed distance from 57th Street or in the fact that the human heart beats with a steady rhythm. There is also orderliness in the regularity with which certain species of birds annually migrate and there certainly is orderliness in the scientific finding, for example, that the volume, the temperature and the pressure of a gas have a fixed relationship.

2. See the Section, "Determinism Versus Indeterminism," pp. 65-70.

3. Physical entities differ from one another with respect to the degree and level of their internal stability (intrinsic unchangeableness). Thus on the *macrocosmic* level solid objects are generally more stable — notably with respect to their shape and size — than free-flowing liquid or gaseous entities. But on one or more of the microcosmic levels (that is, the molecular or atomic or sub-atomic level) virtually all physical entities — or rather their ultimate or penultimate constituents — have a maximal degree of internal stability. The stability on the macrocosmic level enables us to formulate laws (for example, the law of gravitation) concerning macrocosmic interactions; the stability on the microcosmic level enables us to

formulate laws (for example, the laws of chemistry) concerning microcosmic interactions.

4. Relative motion (i.e., motion in relation to some external entity) is a "non-intrinsic" (derivative) property of an entity; temperature in relation to gravity, is a "causally non-relevant" property.

5. It needs to be borne in mind that a property which remains "unchanged or essentially unchanged" may, in a secondary sense, involve a great deal of change — for example, the property, possessed by a radioactive substance, of disintegrating at a fixed rate.

6. Perhaps special reference should be made to the orderliness or patternization which is inherent in the fact that organisms are, in an impressive degree, functionally adapted to their environments. Here too determinism and property persistence serve to promote orderliness but it is the various specific properties of living entities and of the entities in their environment which make for this *particular form* of orderliness.

FUSION AND SEPARATION IN RELATION TO WORLD HISTORY

In another Section,[1] reference is made to a Fusion (or Love) Principle and to a Separation (or Hate) Principle. The former is defined in terms of the tendency of living organisms to increase contact with what is vitalizing, the latter in terms of the tendency of living organisms to decrease contact with what is devitalizing. In this Section I wish (a) to propose a "theory of world history" which may be applicable, among other areas,[2] to the socio-cultural history of Man and to the mass-energy history of the universe and (b) to relate that theory to the Fusion and Separation Principles. Let me hasten to add, and to emphasize, that I am fully aware that my thinking in this Section, particularly in regard to the applicability of the Fusion and Separation Principles, is, at the least, highly speculative.

The theory of history which I wish to propose is the following: *that given any appropriate socio-cultural or mass-energy or other system, there is a long term tendency for the differences within that system to diminish in degree (in a manner suggestive of the Fusion Principle) and to increase in number and variety (in a manner suggestive of the Separation Principle).* Let me cite some of the considerations I have in mind.

(1) (a) It seems to be an accepted sociological fact that socio-cultural traits, whether material (e.g., technological) or ideational, given a relatively open-ended (fluid) socio-cultural system within which they have a relatively high degree of functionality (usefulness), tend to spread throughout that system — in other words, that with the passage of time, a trait which was present in only *one* socio-cultural

context within such a system is likely to be found in some *other* socio-cultural context in that system as well. In the light of this fact we may say that the degree of difference between the two contexts is likely to be reduced or, in my terminology, that there is a tendency for socio-cultural differences to *diminish in degree.*

(1) (b) It also seems to be an accepted sociological fact that, given the aforementioned systematic conditions, socio-cultural traits, whether material (e.g., technological) or ideational, tend to break down into a number of qualitatively different sub-traits, in brief, to become differentiated. It is on this basis that I speak of the tendency for socio-cultural differences to *increase in number and variety.*[3]

(2) (a) According to the Second Law of Thermodynamics, energy which exists in relatively organized (available) forms tends to be transformed into less organized (available) forms. Thus the law suggests that, with the passage of sufficient time, all differences in the degree of energy organization (availability) will disappear. Twentieth century physics has found it necessary to restate this law with the view to embracing within it numerous apparent exceptions, but at least a general trend in the direction of the degradation of energy is still accepted as a scientific fact. The existence of such a trend would give substantial support to the theory of history I have set forth, that is, so far as that theory pertains to differences *in degree* within a mass-energy system. What of differences *in number and variety?*

(2) (b) That the physical universe in which we live is, or at least appears to be, expanding is also widely accepted as a scientific fact, although much is obscure as to the "reasons" for this apparent trend and though the possibility of a counter-trend, periodic or otherwise, can by no means be excluded. If we conceive of this universal expansion as having resulted from, or at least as being analogous to, a

primordial explosion of some sort, it becomes reasonable to view the process of expansion as entailing a coordinate process of fragmentation and differentiation. It seems clear that such a view of the universe would lend support to what I have said in regard to an increase in the *number and variety* of differences within a mass-energy system.

Let us pass on now from the scientific considerations which have been briefly cited in the preceding paragraphs and relate these to the Fusion and Separation Principles. I have noted that both on a socio-cultural level and on a mass-energy level, there appears to be a long-term tendency toward both diffusion and differentiation. But insofar as diffusion occurs, is not the moving out into the surrounding area somewhat analogous to the moving out of an organism toward a vitalizing stimulus object? And insofar as differentiation occurs, is not the separation process somewhat analogous to an organism's separating itself from a devitalizing stimulus object? With appropriate emphasis on the qualifying term "somewhat," I would answer these questions in the affirmative.

Is it possible that something *more* is operative here than a rough analogy? That is, is it possible that the Fusion and Separation Principles are ontologically *real* and that in some way they actually serve to *bring about* the diffusion and the differentiation? Such a metaphysical hypothesis is not without its grandiose appeal. But if it is not demonstrably false, neither is there sufficient evidence to support it. For the present, therefore, if a bit regretfully, I must consider the Fusion and Separation Principles to possess merely the linguistic, which is to say the fictional, reality of scientific metaphors.

1. "The Basic Forms of Response," p. 15.

2. For example, the area of organic evolution.

3. What, more specifically, are some of the socio-cultural implications of my suggested theory of history? Let us consider, for example, the matter of linguistics. What we can expect in this regard, apparently, is the

continuing exportation of certain previously localized forms of expression and the continuing multiplication of forms of expression. Or consider the matter of technology. What we can anticipate here, apparently, is the continuing dissemination of various technological advances and more and more technological refinements.

PHILOSOPHICAL DESCRIPTIVISM: PROPOSITIONS, MEANINGS AND ENTAILMENT

When a dog has learned that the sounding of a bell "means" that food is available at a certain spot, few, if any, philosophers would say that a full description of what occurs when he is responding to what he hears requires that we take into consideration some "proposition" (in the sense of some kind of extra-organismic entity, not identical with a sentence,[1] but which has, or is, a meaning) which the dog is thinking about or is maintaining or is asserting to be true. Exactly what *is* occurring is not easily describable; it involves the activation of complicated neurological and associated events and (under certain circumstances) an overt behavioral response. But it does not, certainly, involve any such "proposition."

It seems to me equally clear that no such "proposition" is involved in the responses of human beings, whether they be non-verbal responses like going to the dining room to eat, or verbal responses like saying "I usually have breakfast in the dining room." The situation is the same when I make a "philosophical" assertion – for example, that "Beauty is objective" or that "Dialectical Materialism is inconsistent with Free Will." To be sure, I may be uttering certain *sounds* or making certain *marks* on a piece of paper and the neurological and associated events, and perhaps the behavioral response, may be more complicated. But that is all.

Many philosophers, however, but not *only* philosophers, have somehow come to think that such "propositions," and the "concepts" which constitute them, are *existents*, if not actual parts of the real world in which we live, then at least existents of *some* sort; and they have concerned themselves with the "meaning" and with the "truth" or "falsity" of various "propositions" and with their "logical relationships" to one another. "Propositions" — and "concepts" too, including mathematical concepts — thus get to be discussed as if they were semi-real "objects" whose properties and interrelationships are "there" to be discovered and illuminated. *It is as if we had only to look at them sufficiently closely, to inspect them sufficiently carefully, to discover the true nature of each of these objects — that is, what each of the propositions or concepts "really" amounts to, what each "really" means. This fallacy, I believe, accounts for much of the endless controversy which has plagued philosophy throughout its history.*

Suppose we are concerned about the "content" or "object" or "datum" of perception and that the question before us is: "In veridical human perception, do we perceive a sense datum or a physical object?" In my judgment, we will be bogged down in hopeless confusion if in seeking to answer this question we attempt to "analyze the meaning" of various "propositions" relating to what we perceive (where the term "proposition" is employed in the sense indicated above). For such "propositions" simply are non-existent.[2] Moreover, if our purpose is to "analyze meanings" I should think that it would be only reasonable to direct ourselves to the settings in which meanings actually occur — that is, to an actual response or responses made by an actual person or persons — and not to some highly conventionalized (not to say non-existent) entity which at best can only very indirectly "express" what was actually meant.

How, then, can we proceed in relation to this philosophical question? What we can do here, and what we can do in relation to any *other* philosophical question, is to try to describe[3] (illuminate, clarify, etc.) *what it is that we believe occurs.* Thus we can try to describe, for example, *what it is that we believe occurs* in connection with the *act* or *response* or *process* which is called (by us or certain other persons) "perceiving," that is to say, what it is that *takes place* when we are perceiving. (In regard to this, see the Section, "Epistemological Monism Versus Epistemological Dualism," pp. 53-55.) Or we can try to describe, for example, *what it is that we believe occurs* in connection with the *use* (by us or certain other persons) *of the term* "perceiving," that is to say, what is *meant* by "perceiving." In other words, we may seek to deal with the problem either by setting forth some *non-linguistic* descriptive statements about perception or, as a number of contemporary linguistic philosophers do, by setting forth some *linguistic* descriptive statements about perception.[4] Neither of *these* approaches, unlike the "propositional" approach, need lead us into a direction-less world of unreality from which we cannot extricate ourselves.

Similar remarks apply to a long list of other philosophical questions ranging from "What is the nature of virtue?" to "What is the nature of time?"

Consider, for example, the Socratic question concerning the essence of virtue. If we examine the "concept" of virtue as if it were some kind of "object" whose essential nature (meaning) is "there" to be discovered and laid bare, we will sink into a semantic quagmire. However here too we can direct ourselves toward describing (illuminating, clarifying, etc.) *what it is that we believe occurs.* Thus, for example, we can try to describe *what it is that we believe occurs* when people conduct themselves in a way which is regarded (by us or certain other persons) as revealing "virtue". Or we can try to describe, for example, *what it is that we believe occurs* in connection with the use (by us or certain other persons) of the word "virtue," what it is that we believe some person or persons, in some context or other, may "mean" by that term.

There are a number of philosophical questions which are, or which involve, questions about *logical relationships*, questions about logical relationships between "propositions" or about logical relationships between "concepts." Thus we may have such questions as "Does ethical guilt entail ethical responsibility?" or "Can a Logical Positivist be a Metaphysical Dualist?" or "Is Fatalism inconsistent with Determinism?", questions which are of, or are reducible to, the form "Does A entail B?"[5] Here too we are headed for trouble if, presuming that A and B have some sort of objective (extra-organismic) existence, we seek to find out what it is that A really means and what it is that B really means and then to see if A does or does not entail B. We also *may* encounter difficulties if we limit ourselves to exploring whether *if* A means such-and-such and *if B* means such-and-such, A entails (or does not entail) B. For here too we *may* be *objectifying* meanings, that is, we may be presuming that, like the alleged "propositions" or "concepts" to which they are "attached," or which they "constitute," they have some kind of objective (extra-organismic) existence. We may not be limiting ourselves to describing *what it is that we believe is occurring* (or has occurred or will occur) *in the real world in which we live.*

To be sure, when we say that *if* we mean such-and-such by A and *if* we mean such-and-such by B *then* A entails B, we are saying something that seems to make sense and that seems to be valid or invalid. How is this possible if we are asserting a relationship between non-existents? This *is* possible in virtue of the fact that we more or less have in mind an *analogous* relationship between *real* entities within the *real* world in which we live. There, if M and N exist, N must exist; that is, if a whole (in the sense of a collection) exists, a part of that whole (a member of that collection) must exist. *Thus "entailment' is merely an analogue, so to speak, of physical inclusion; and it is only in virtue of that analogy that assertions that one "proposition" or "concept" or "meaning" entails some other "proposition" or "concept" or "meaning" seem to make sense and appear to be either valid or invalid.*

I would like to refer to the philosophical position which

has been set forth and espoused in this Section as "Philosophical Descriptivism" and hence to myself as a "Philosophical Descriptivist." But I would wish it understood that in speaking of my "philosophical position," I am not presuming that it is a set of "propositions," "concepts" or "meanings" having some sort of objective existence. What that "position" comes down to is merely a set of highly complicated dispositional (attitudinal) responses on my part to the real world in which I live.

In the light of what has been said in this Section, it is apparent that *for the Descriptivist the only feasible object (subject matter) of philosophical inquiry is the universe in which we live. For there is no metaexistential world of objective "essences" or "concepts" or "propositions" or "meanings," etc.* In the view of the Descriptivist, therefore, those from Plato to Wittgenstein who have proposed that such a world (or some particular segment of it) be set aside as the philosopher's special domain have in effect proposed his disinheritance!

1. By a "sentence" I mean a certain combination of pre-defined marks, sounds, etc. having a particular space-time locus — e.g., a locus on this page.

2. That is, they are not present (do not have position) in public space and/or time or in so called "private" space and/or time. See the Section, "The Definition of Existence and Reality," pp. 74-77.

3. In this connection, see the Section which follows.

4. We may, of course, do both.

5. "Entailment" (sometimes called "necessary implication") is a "basic" logical relationship to which certain other logical relationships — for example, "being consistent with" — can be "reduced." Thus if A does not entail non-B, A is "consistent with" B.

DESCRIPTION, CORRESPONDENCE AND TRUTH

In the preceding Section, I have written about "describing" what is occurring (or has occurred or will occur). Now when we are engaged in "describing," as when we are engaged in any other act of communication, we are engaged in producing certain sensory stimuli or stimulation sources (for example, certain marks or sounds) which normally are calculated to activate, given certain conditions, a certain kind of response on the part of some (actual or possible) subject. The sensory stimuli or stimulation sources may vary over a wide range and they may or may not consist of those marks or sounds, etc. which go to make up words.

A great many philosophers have maintained that something (sometimes identified as a "proposition," sometimes as an "assertion," sometimes as a "statement," sometimes as a "sentence," sometimes as a "belief," etc.) is true when it *corresponds* with the fact to which it refers and false when it does *not* correspond (or when it "dis-corresponds") with that fact. I have long felt, however, that this contention, though on the surface, perhaps, both clear and reasonable, is actually neither.

In the first place, an inanimate entity — certainly a non-existent inanimate entity — cannot in and of itself "refer" to anything, any more than an inanimate entity (say, a chair or the universe) can have a goal or a purpose or an aim. Only an animate entity (e.g., a human being) can "refer" to something, though an inanimate entity (e.g., a set of marks) can, of course, serve to induce an animate entity to refer to something or serve, very indirectly, to "record" some act of reference by an animate entity. And still more obviously, only an animate entity can think about or believe or doubt or judge, etc. something.

In the second place, the "correspondence" which allegedly characterizes the relationship between a true proposition or assertion or statement or sentence or belief, etc., on the one hand, and the fact to which it refers, on the other hand, is, in my view, illusory. For in order for the relationship of "correspondence," or for any other relationship, to be present, *the terms of that relationship must be real, must be existents.*[1] But if by a "proposition" or "assertion," etc. we *do* mean some existent (say, a set of marks or some occurrence within someone's head), and if by a "fact" we mean some other existent (say, some actual occurrence or state of affairs in the real world), the required "correspondence," in the broad sense of a qualitative or structural resemblance of some sort, is completely lacking. To be specific: if I assert that New York City has a population of over 7,000,000 people, there simply is no qualitative or structural resemblance whatever between the *words* I may use, or anything that may occur in my head when I use them, and the people in New York themselves.

For my own part, I would prefer not to speak of any proposition or assertion or statement, etc. as being "true" or "false" unless it is clearly recognized (as I hope it now will be!) that I regard this form of expression as very much of a short-cut – linguistically convenient, perhaps, but philosophically quite likely to be confusing. *I believe it would be much more precise, if much more cumbersome, to speak rather, for example, of what responses, in the way of negative or affirmative judgments (beliefs), are elicited, or are deemed by certain persons to be likely to be elicited, by certain sensory stimuli or stimulation sources – specifically, certain kinds of marks, sounds, etc. – under certain conditions, in some (actual or potential) subjects.*[2] For in and of itself, that is, without regard to the responses it may elicit, a set of marks (e.g., the marks, "the Earth is flat") or a set of sounds, etc. can no more appropriately be called "true" or "false" than can any other existent – e.g., a chair or a neurophysiological event or a sonata – and to call a *non-existent* entity "true" or "false" is likely to involve one, if one is not already involved, in metaphysical nonsense!

1. See the Section, "The Definition of Existence and Reality," pp. 76-77.

2. This more elaborate form of expression would *not* require us to accept a "relativistic" view of truth, in the sense that the truth or falsity of a proposition or assertion or statement, etc. (e.g., that "the Earth is flat" or that "Picasso is a great artist") would necessarily vary from time to time in accordance with shifts in people's responses (judgments). For our point of reference could well be some *fixed and unchanging* response or responses (judgments), e.g., the response (judgment) which certain specified persons *would* make under certain specified conditions, for example, if they were completely knowledgeable.

PSYCHICAL ENTITIES

In the Section, "Substance, Property Complexes and Scientific Realism," I indicated that the notion that a physical entity is something (for example, a physical substance) which has or possesses certain properties is untenable and I suggested that we conceive of a physical entity instead as consisting of the *properties themselves,* that is, as a *property complex.* The criticism presented there, however, also has relevance to the view that a *non-physical,* that is, a *psychical,* entity is something (for example, a psychical substance) which has or possesses certain properties. Nor does it matter, of course, whether we are considering the "mind" or the "self" or the "ego" or "psychic energy" or "consciousness" or any other presumably non-physical entity.

Suppose, though, one were to meet this objection and were to regard the "mind" or "self" or "ego," etc. as a property complex of some sort rather than as a property-less "it" which possesses certain properties. Could I then agree that at least some of these terms, as commonly defined, denote non-physical entities which *exist?* As I have indicated elsewhere,[1] it is my view that the only non-physical or psychical entities which *exist,* in other words, which are present either in public or private space-time, are stimulation indicators, that is, (the subjective components of) sights, sounds, tastes, odors, tactile sensations, other bodily sensations and images. All other existents are *physical* entities. Thus if in asserting the existence of the mind or self, etc. one is asserting the existence of anything *other* than (some combination of) stimulation indicators and/or physical entities, I would maintain that one is *claiming* existence for what *does not in fact have* existence.

For a great many philosophers and psychologists, however, the world of psychical, or non-physical, entities is much more heavily populated.

One of the most notable of these entities is the "ego." Long prominent in philosophy as a unitary entity more or less identical with the popular notion of the self, the ego also found a place for itself in the emerging systems of modern psychology. For the psychoanalytic psychologist, however, the ego – sometimes called the "personality" – became a tripartite entity consisting of the id, the ego proper and the superego; and he soon began talking of "strong" egos and of "weak" egos, of "healthy" egos and of "neurotic" egos, etc. as well. Do any or all of these "egos" exist?

To be sure, an ego, unitary or tripartite, strong or weak, etc. *can* be defined, as can any *other* entity, of course, in terms of what *does* exist, what *actually occurs* – for example, in terms of certain neurological events or in terms of certain specified kinds of responses made under certain specified kinds of circumstances. But if an ego *is* defined in this way, it is extremely difficult, indeed impossible, to see how it can fulfill its designated role, that is, how it can be the kind of entity which can perform the various tasks or functions as a directing or mediating "agent" which are customarily assigned to it. The fact is, moreover, that an ego, unitary or tripartite, strong or weak, etc. is usually conceived, not in such *mundane* terms but as a *transcendental* entity, as an entity which lacks a determinable location within the body yet which in some mysterious way nonetheless guides, directs or controls a wide variety of personal responses. Certainly, so conceived, the ego is as unreal as an evil spirit or as Satan himself.[2]

The objections which I have raised here in regard to the notion of an "ego" are also applicable, with suitable modifications, to a long list of similar concepts, for example, the "superego",[3] the "censor," the "id," the "libido," the "self," the "soul," etc. *In other words, defined in terms of existents, they are unable to fulfill their assigned roles but left as transcendental entities, they remain unreal.*

Perhaps the entity (apart from the "content" of experience) whose psychical reality is most widely accepted in professional circles is "consciousness." In my judgment, however, the existence of a psychical "consciousness" is also illusory.

Let us consider in turn the two major senses in which the word is used.

(1) Sometimes when we use the term "consciousness", we are referring to an overall *condition* or *state.* Thus we may speak of a state of "consciousness" in contrast to a state of "unconsciousness" (or of not being conscious), meaning by the latter the kind of state we are in when we have fainted or have fallen asleep. But it seems to me clear that the difference which is to be noted between these two conditions or states does not at all require us to suppose that a psychical entity corresponding to the term "consciousness" is present in the former case and absent in the latter – any more than it requires us to suppose that a psychical entity corresponding to the term "unconsciousness" is *absent* in the former case and *present* in the latter! What the difference between these two states comes down to is simply a difference in the operation of our neurophysiological apparatus and a consequent difference in some of our responses, most obviously our overt responses. (In a state of unconsciousness, even stimulation indicators – e.g., dream images – may continue to occur.)

(2) At other times when we speak of "consciousness," we are referring to a particular contrast *within the state of consciousness itself.* This is the contrast between *having consciousness of something* – e.g., of the sounds coming from the adjoining room – and *being conscious but not having consciousness of that something.*[4] I would say that the difference here, however, is simply a difference between

attending to something and *not attending* to that something, a difference which is associated with the manner in which we organize or structure our perceptual or cognitive field. When we begin to focus our attention on something, we are, perceptually or cognitively, *turning toward* that something and thereby, in accordance with the BT, maximizing the stimulation that something is eliciting in us. We are increasing its impact upon us.[5] But here too, it seems clear, what is taking place does *not* include the coming into existence of any *special kind* of psychical, or non-physical, entity – that is, any psychical, or non-physical, entity other than a stimulation indicator – whether we choose to describe the matter in terms of "consciousness" or "attentiveness" or "perception" or in some other way.[6]

It remains for me to say a few words about the ontological status of those "everyday" entities sometimes identified as constituting the "cognitive or emotional content" of experience, such entities as "thoughts," "ideas," "desires," "fears," "beliefs," "attitudes," etc. To what extent, if at all, does *their* occurrence involve the presence of something psychical, i.e., non-physical? Let me take as representative examples "thoughts," "fears" and "attitudes."

When I am having a certain "thought" (say, about the appointments which have been scheduled for me for the following day), what is actually taking place, I would say, consists of the occurrence of certain highly complicated neurophysiological changes (which of course are physical) and of the occurrence of certain bodily sensations (perhaps vague anticipatory feelings of one sort or another) and certain images (say, of the people I expect to see or of the notations I may have observed in my appointment book). Only the bodily sensations and the images, or rather their subjective components, are non-physical (psychical); that is to say, only they have reality but are not in public space-time.

When I am experiencing a feeling of "fear" (say, in

connection with having been narrowly missed by an automobile), the situation, ontologically speaking, is exactly the same. Here, however, the neurophysiological changes are precipitated primarily by a highly charged perceptual situation, the neurophysiological and behavioral changes induced are more marked, the accompanying bodily sensations are more intense and of a more negative quality, and the accompanying images more vivid.

Nor is the situation ontologically different when I am said to have a certain "attitude" (e.g., a hostile attitude toward a particular individual). Here the central, the defining, factor is the presence of a more or less persistent response tendency which is rooted in my body mechanism [7] and which, when I am subjected to certain stimuli, results in my feeling, and otherwise reacting, toward the individual in a particular (i.e., hostile) way. But here too the only *psychical* entities present are the subjective components of my bodily sensations and of my images. In other words, here too *the "content" of our experience involves, in addition to the causally related physical entities, only those non-physical (psychical) entities which I have termed "stimulation indicators."*

It is a well-established socio-anthropological fact that for many thousands of years Man has populated his world with all kinds of non-existent entities, from demons and evil spirits to protective mythological heroes and immortal gods. But in my judgment the propensity to create such fictional entities is also manifesting itself today. Thus even within the relatively cautious conceptualizations of contemporary physics, we find repeated references to gravitational, electromagnetic and various other kinds of operating "forces." In relation to the study of human behavior, it is probably the psychoanalyst who is especially guilty of such unwarranted postulations, maintaining as he does the reality of a vast array of non-physical entities ranging from unconscious minds to libidinal energy. I would like to suggest that Man's continuing propensity to overpopulate his world in this way is a reflection of his continuing need (i.e., tendency) to *animate* his world, a need which, despite certain inhibitory factors in contemporary society, is apparently as compelling as ever. An analysis of this need (tendency) and of some of its multiple ramifications will be found elsewhere.[8]

1. See the Section, "Metaphysical Dualism," pp. 56-57. In connection with the present Section, see also, "The Nature of Psychological Responses," pp. 103-104, and "Do We Have An Unconscious Mind?", pp. 105-108.

2. Freud described the ego as performing a "mediating function" in relation to reality. Yet inconsistently he sometimes regarded the ego not as something real, but merely as a convenient scientific construct. I say "inconsistently" since obviously a scientific construct can do or affect nothing. Let me also point out, what Freud seems at times to have forgotten, that it is one thing to identify the ego with a mediating *purpose* or *task* or *role,* etc., and still another to identify it with that *which directs* these responses or *which has* this purpose or task or role, etc.

3. In my view, the inhibition of a response is brought about by the DV stimulation which is elicited by the anticipation, or by the incipient activation, of that response, *not* by any "censor" or "superego." See the Section, "Guilt," pp. 151-152.

4. When we speak of being "conscious" or "aware" of something, we sometimes simply mean that we *already have knowledge* of that something. But *this* use of the term has never raised any *metaphysical* problems, that is, has never been construed to imply the existence of consciousness or awareness as a distinct psychical entity of some sort.

5. When we shift our attention from A to B, it is because B, at least when we have begun to attend to it, is becoming more *vitalizing* to us. See the Section, "The Vitalizing Effect of Stimulation Per Se", pp. 17-18.

6. The history of philosophy contains the long standing suggestion that consciousness is analogous to a searchlight which shifts its illuminative focus from one area to another. However in my view this analogy is grossly misleading for there *is* no psychical searchlight. There is merely a shift in our perceptual or cognitive content, in what (to change the analogy) we *tune in on.* The error here is somewhat like the error of supposing that motion exists because moving objects exist.

7. See the following Section, "The Nature of Psychological Responses."

8. See the Section, "Animism, Psychopathology and Devitalization," pp. 133-139.

PART FOUR

ON FREUD AND THE UNCONSCIOUS

THE NATURE OF PSYCHOLOGICAL RESPONSES[1]

Every physical object has a composition and structure in virtue of which, when it is acted upon in a certain manner, it will react in one particular way rather than in some other. (For example, a piece of paper, when placed in contact with a flame, will, under normal conditions, burn rather than melt; a piece of steel, when immersed in water, will, under normal conditions, sink rather than float.) This statement applies no less to animate objects, including the bodies of human beings, than it does to inanimate objects. Thus every physical object, inanimate or animate, may be said to possess, in virtue of its composition and structure, its own particular set of *response possibilities,* its own particular *response potential.*[2] (This concept is employed in connection with some observations made in the following Section concerning an "unconscious mind.")

In describing the behavior of certain types of animate objects, particularly the behavior of human beings and members of other relatively "advanced" species, it is customary to refer to some of their forms of response, such as hoping, getting angry, believing, remembering, anticipating, thinking, dreaming, etc., as "psychological." Such "psychological" responses are often conceived to be in some way "less physical" or "more non-physical" than so-called "physiological" responses, say, breathing, sneezing, digesting, urinating, belching, sleeping, moving about, etc. In my view, however, this is an error. For the only non-physical *existents* are stimulation indicators and these may be present in connection with "physiological" as well as "psychological" responses. Indeed, stimulation indicators – for example, acute bodily sensations – may at times be very *vividly* present in relation to certain "physiological" processes, whereas in relation to certain "psychological" processes, say, certain kinds of remembering or anticipating or thinking, stimulation indicators may be virtually or totally absent.

It is not being asserted here, of course, that there are *no* differences between "physiological" and "psychological" responses. The contention is rather that such differences as we may find are *non-ontological,* that is, do not involve any characteristic difference with respect to the absence or presence of something which is non-physical.[3]

1. In connection with this Section and the following one, see the Sections, "Metaphysical Dualism," pp. 56-61, and "Psychical Entities," pp. 95-100.

2. The term "response" is used in this paragraph in a broader sense than that indicated in the Section, "The Basic Tendency," p. 8, being here applied to inanimate as well as animate entities.

3. A number of writers have alleged that explanation of a given act in terms of a particular intention or purpose or motive, etc. is irreconcilable with its explanation in neurophysiological terms. But in my view there is *not* any incompatibility between the two since an intention, etc., apart from any stimulation indicators which it may involve, *is* neurophysiological, that is, consists of behavior-affecting neurophysiological components. Nor is either incompatible with explanation in terms of the BT; each is a different type or level of "explanation".

DO WE HAVE AN UNCONSCIOUS MIND?[1]

When my brain – or rather my nervous system – is being stimulated in a certain way, certain entities which I have called "psychical" or "non-physical" are present. These are "stimulation indicators" and consist, as previously indicated, of (the subjective components of) sights, sounds, odors, tastes, tactile sensations, other bodily sensations and images. In my view, no other psychical (non-physical) entities ever occur and these occur only when and so long as my nervous system (or some other nervous system) is appropriately stimulated. Yet those who speak of an "unconscious mind" often seem to believe that each of us, in addition, perhaps, to a psychical *apparatus* (involving, say, a "self" or "ego"), carries around, unnoticed by him and, in any direct way, unnoticeable, a variegated psychical *content*, a content consisting of emotions, feelings, attitudes, desires, fears, thoughts, memories, etc. – and that these unconscious entities, moreover, may significantly influence our behavior. This is a view which I cannot at all accept.

What each of us *does* "carry around," I would say, is a highly complex and intricate body mechanism whose controlling center is the brain. And if person A responds to a given stimulus situation differently from person B, this is the result of a *present physical* difference in their body mechanisms. Thus if there is any truth in the statement, for example, that A has an "unconscious hatred" of his father and that B does *not* have an "unconscious hatred" of *his* father, this involves a *present physical* difference in their body mechanisms, a present physical difference of such a nature that, if and when A and B are confronted with certain stimulus situations (for example, situations relating to their fathers or father figures or authority figures or men, etc.) they will respond in different ways deemed to be confirmatory of the hypothesis. In brief, what A carries around, so far as his "unconscious hatred" is concerned, is a body mechanism having *a certain particular response potential. He does not carry around any psychical (non-physical) entity associated with the hatred of his father, but only the potential to react with hatred, or in some other way deemed to confirm the hypothesis, when he is confronted with certain stimulus situations. Only when he actually does react with hatred is there anything psychical present which is connected with the hatred; and the hatred-connected psychical element then present is limited to stimulation indicators, in particular to (the subjective components of) bodily sensations (including feelings of anger) and images.*

What has been said here of an unconscious hatred of one's father applies equally, of course, to any other unconscious emotion or feeling or attitude – in fact, to the whole gamut of unconscious entities which are supposed by some to exist in, or to constitute, a so-called "unconscious mind". And its validity is in no way contingent upon whether we are considering the "unconscious mind" of someone awake or asleep or whether, if asleep, he is dreaming or not dreaming.

If, for example, someone is asleep and is having a dream which may "express" his unconscious hatred of his father, what is taking place is limited to the occurrence of certain neurophysiological events, certain dream images and certain bodily sensations, the particular nature of these occurrences being dependent on the particular nature of the body mechanism, in other words, its particular response potential. The bodily sensations and the dream images (or rather, their subjective components) are, of course, stimulation indicators, like the (subjective components of the) bodily sensations and the images and the sights and the sounds, etc. which may occur when one is awake; and like other stimulation indicators, they are correlated with certain physical events in the brain. But nothing else of a psychical nature — no persistent psychical entity which might be called "unconscious hatred" — is present. *Ontologically speaking, that is the entire story.*

The concept of an "unconscious mind" which has been outlined here is quite different, of course, from Freud's. It does not presuppose the existence of any kind of psychical (non-physical) self (or ego or id or superego) which is the "subject" of certain experiences or which performs certain functions, nor does it presuppose that we carry around in our "unconscious" a vast collection of continuing-to-exist psychical entities which might be called emotions, feelings, attitudes, desires, fears, thoughts, memories, etc.[2]

In relation to the latter thesis, let me say that my rejection of it rests not only on the fact that *it is a completely gratuitous and unnecessary supposition,* not to say *one which is operationally meaningless,* but also on the fact that *it is open to a serious epistemological objection,* an objection which seemingly has been almost universally overlooked. If their attention were directed to the matter, those accepting the Freudian thesis would doubtless concede that in sensing (seeing, hearing, etc.) or in having an image, the psychical entities which occur (which I have called "stimulation indicators") depend for their existence upon the concomitant, or immediately antecedent, stimulation of the brain — in other words, that *stimulation indicators maintain their existence only so long as the stimulation eliciting them is present.* Yet oblivious to the implications of this significant fact, they have nevertheless presumed that there may be psychical entities connected with emotions, feelings, attitudes, desires, etc. which can somehow continue to exist, supposedly in the "unconscious mind," long after the brain stimulation which once may have elicited them on a "conscious" level has ceased to be present, indeed that many psychical entities can persist in the "unconscious mind" without *ever* having been elicited by such stimulation.

Clearly *there is a complete lack of epistemological consistency here*.

1. In connection with this Section and the preceding one, see the Sections, "Metaphysical Dualism," pp. 56-61, and "Psychical Entities," pp. 95-100.
2. Of course, our bodies *do* "carry around" the neurophysiological changes associated with our *having had* certain feelings, emotions, etc.; our bodies *do* "carry around" certain *response possibilities*.

THE INTERPRETATION OF THE UNCONSCIOUS[1]

When two psychotherapists (I use the term "psychotherapists" in its generic sense to include psychoanalysts as well) disagree as to the correct unconscious level interpretation of a patient's behavior (not excluding, of course, his dreams), that is to say, posit the behind-the-scenes operation of different unconscious psychical entities (motives, feelings, desires, needs, etc.), it is evident that the disagreement cannot be resolved on the basis of their *observing* the alleged unconscious occurrence. The most that a therapist can *observe* is what, over some period of time, the patient *says* and *does* – how he *behaves.* (As a matter of fact, even the patient cannot observe, either through sense perception or through introspection, the alleged unconscious occurrence.)

This fact, in itself, poses no theoretical obstacle to the making of a well-grounded choice between hypotheses. In physics, for example, we are frequently choosing one hypothesis over some alternative hypothesis in spite of the fact that the different entities posited may themselves be unobserved or even, in a sense, theoretically unobservable. Occasionally that choice is made wholly on the basis of certain broad methodological principles.[2] But more typically it is made, at least partly, on the basis of the testable consequences, that is, after noting that whereas the implications of one of the hypotheses are consistent with our observations, the implications of the alternative hypothesis are not. *I suggest, however, that when it comes to competing interpretations involving the postulation of different unconscious psychical entities (motives, feelings, etc.), it is impossible to make a choice on this basis. For such an entity, lacking, as it is conceived, not only the quantitative (i.e., the mathematical) but even the determinate properties of a physical entity, cannot have any clearcut or unambiguous observational consequences; and this difficulty is compounded by the presumption that it operates within a highly mobile and complex psychological network, including the defense mechanisms, which in various unpredictable ways may disguise or transform it. The result is that any observation which is made is reconcilable both with the presence and the absence of such an entity.*[3]

Suppose, for example, we have a school resistant – some might say school phobic – child who is constantly clinging to her mother. In such a case, some therapists might maintain that the girl's behavior in relation to her mother indicates just what it *seems* to indicate, namely, a marked dependency on, and a strong positive feeling for, her mother. Other therapists, however, might maintain that the behavior is a "reaction formation" and thus disguises the girl's "real" feeling for her mother which, at least on the unconscious level, is strongly *negative.*

In support of the view that the child's unconscious feeling toward her mother is strongly *negative,* a therapist might endeavor to demonstrate that, not only in relation to the school situation but in relation to a number of other situations as well, the girl manifests such an *excessive* interest in, concern about, dependence on, or desire to be near her mother that the genuineness of the feeling she displays must, at the very least, be highly suspect. Or he might attempt to show that there are relatively *direct* indications of an underlying negative feeling, for example, in the girl's temper tantrums when her mother is felt to be neglecting her, or in her frequently hostile dreams.

But a therapist who rejects this point of view might argue that the girl's manifestation of a marked interest in, concern about, etc. her mother is just what it appears to be, namely, evidence of a strong *positive* feeling toward her mother, conscious and presumably unconscious too, and that the temper tantrums and other patterns of response alleged to be indicative of an unconscious negative feeling are also otherwise interpretable. Thus he might argue that the temper tantrums, being the result of marked frustration, simply underscore the fact that the girl has a strong *positive* feeling for her mother. And he might argue that the girl's dreams, dreams, let us say, wherein the mother is pictured as ill or dead or ugly, etc., are properly construed to mean, not that she *wishes* these things to happen to her mother, but that she *fears* they will happen to her, or perhaps that she *wishes* them to happen to some *other* mother figure, e.g., to the school teacher whose class she does not wish to attend, or perhaps that she *fears* that they will happen (because she feels guilty about not wanting to "share" her mother) to herself, etc., etc.

We have here, therefore, a situation in which two quite different, indeed "opposite," unconscious psychical entities are presumed to be present but where it seems impossible, on the basis of the available evidence, that is, on the basis of our observations, to determine which of the two entities, if either, actually *is* present. The fundamental reason for this, in this instance as in other instances, has been indicated above, namely, *the fact that the postulated entities are without any unambiguous consequences, a deficiency resulting from the indeterminateness of these entities and from the unpredictable ways in which, through the operation of defense mechanisms and otherwise, they admittedly may be disguised or transformed.*

If psychotherapists who accept the reality of unconscious psychical entities should be unduly troubled by this state of affairs, I would propose, as a purely pragmatic solution, the development of an "official" lexicon or dictionary. Such a volume would "officially," if somewhat arbitrarily, define each allegedly unconscious psychical entity – e.g., unconscious hatred of one's mother – in terms of a very specific set of observable occurrences. Thus by the simple act of consulting this lexicon, interpretative disputes could be quickly and "officially" resolved. (In my view, it should be remembered, the only psychical, that is, non-physical, entities which are real are stimulation indicators and these do *not* constitute or persist in any psychical "unconscious mind." See the three immediately preceding Sections.)

Sometimes therapists who disagree about the content of a patient's "unconscious" have had recourse to a pragmatic argument. Thus it is sometimes contended that if one interpretation (e.g., one positing unconscious love) "works" better (i.e., is therapeutically more effective) than another (e.g., one positing unconscious hatred), this is at least *indirect* or *circumstantial* evidence that the former interpretation is valid and the latter invalid. It may be pointed out by way of reply, however, that though, given a particular context, one interpretation undoubtedly *would* work better than another, this fact in no way entails the conclusion which is drawn. An interpretation implying the successful exorcism of an evil spirit may, in some cultures, prove to be highly effective but this hardly demostrates that the patient was actually possessed by such a spirit. I would be more prepared to hold that the effectiveness of an interpretation depends upon what the patient *believes* to be true, though its effectiveness also depends, of course, on a great many other factors, for example, *when* the interpretation is presented, in what *terms* it is presented, *how* it is presented, the patient's "transference," etc., etc.

There is a further comment in regard to interpretation which may be worth adding. This is the point, obvious but frequently ignored, that virtually every interpretation, whether of the "unconscious" or of the "conscious," presupposes a vastly *oversimplified* view of the patient's psychological functioning. For just how a patient, or anyone else, responds in a given situation is apt to be the consequence, of course, not of any *single* experience he has had, or even of any *single strand* of experiences (for example, of his breast feeding or toilet training or sibling rivalry or authority figure experiences) but rather of an indefinitely large number of interlocking and interacting strands of experience, as well as of a multiplicity of independently operating organic factors. Thus interpretation as commonly employed in psychotherapy rests upon a premise which fails to do justice to the vast complexity of the psychogenic facts.

1. For the purposes of this Section, I shall not question the view that there are unconscious psychical (non-physical) entities (feelings, motives, desires, etc.) which constitute, or which persist in, a psychical entity which may be called "an unconscious mind." However, see the three immediately preceding Sections.

2. Such as their relative plausibility or their relative simplicity or their relative coherence with accepted hypotheses, etc.

3. Let me mention in passing that if we assume that our observations concerning someone's (physical) behavior yield some information concerning that person's psychical content, conscious or unconscious, we are making this *philosophical* presupposition, namely, that the psychical must in some degree *influence*, or at least *be correlated with*, the physical. See the Section, "Psychophysical Interactionism," pp. 62-64.

WHAT WE "REALLY" ARE

It seems to be widely assumed in psychoanalytic circles that one's unconscious wishes, feelings, attitudes, motives, etc. – and for the purposes of this Section the existence of psychical entities of this sort will not be questioned – in contrast to those which are conscious, reflect or express one's "true" nature, that it is these which indicate or characterize what one "really" is. Presumably it is as if there were two different photographs of a person, one of which is a more faithful representation than the other. This is a position, however, which, even if we accept the reality of such unconscious wishes, feelings, etc., seems to me to be confused and open to challenge.

For what exactly is it, supposedly, that *constitutes* one's "true" or "real" nature? What exactly is it with which one's *unconscious* wishes, etc. correspond more accurately than one's *conscious* wishes, etc.? Apparently it is *not* being said that this third entity either is one's *behavior* (either the totality of one's behavior or some sample of it) or the *physical body* (or some part of it) which *does* the behaving. No; what presumably is being asserted is that this third entity (that is, one's "true" or "real" nature) is one's "true" or "real" *self;* and this self apparently is conceived to be some kind of non-physical (psychical) entity which each person is or possesses, perhaps in a somewhat changing form, throughout (at least most of) his life. *This ontological assumption, however, strikes me as being, at best, highly fanciful.* (As already noted,[1] in my view the only non-physical entities which exist are stimulation indicators.)

The position under consideration appears to be supported by two contentions which, for convenience of reference, may be called the "spatial" thesis and the "causal" thesis. Let us consider these in turn.

The spatial thesis is that unconscious wishes, feelings, attitudes, motives, etc. occur "at a much deeper level," "much further below the surface," than conscious ones and hence express much more truly the "fundamental character" of an individual. But in a *literal* sense, of course, so-called unconscious wishes, etc. are no "deeper" within the body or within the "personality" (which can hardly be regarded as spatial at all) than conscious wishes, etc.; and even if they were, the conclusion which is drawn would by no means follow. For clearly an interior segment of an object, however "deep" within the object it may be, need be no more indicative of, or characteristic of, the total object, or of what that object "truly" or "really" is, than a segment which is on the surface.

The causal thesis which seems to be used supportively is that our unconscious wishes, feelings, attitudes, motives, etc., in contrast to our conscious ones, though they may manifest themselves at times in certain disguised and distorted forms, nonetheless remain, in and of themselves, free and undistorted and thus are more genuinely self-representative. But here again it is apparently being assumed that there exists some kind of a non-physical self with which it is possible to make comparisons. Moreover we must remember that any wishes, feelings, attitudes, motives, etc. which one may have are of necessity dependent upon, and hence influenced by, the particular nature of one's neurophysiological apparatus (i.e., one's body mechanism). Thus if the psychoanalyst is presuming that somehow one's unconscious wishes, etc. can *escape* that influence and exist in a state of "pristine purity," so to speak, he is blandly disregarding the epistemological facts.

1. See the Section, "Psychical Entities," pp. 95-100.

SLEEP IN RELATION TO THE BT[1]

Sleep (i.e., natural sleep) may be viewed as a withdrawing (minimizing) response in virtue of which the body has an opportunity to dissipate the state of bodily fatigue which induces it. Its presence serves to reduce the impact of stimulation which would interfere with that opportunity.

Such interference is apt to be brought about by stimulation which is quite strong (intense), for example, stimulation associated with a sharp pain or a loud noise. For such stimulation, in consequence of its momentary *vitalizing* effect, however devitalizing it may be in the long run, is apt to evoke, among organisms capable of sleeping, an attention-giving (alerting) response. And giving attention to a pain or a noise, which is a way of *maximizing* the stimulation associated with that pain or noise, conflicts, of course, with *minimizing* the stimulation associated with that pain or noise.

An antithetical response is also apt to be elicited by an appreciable positive change in the sleep-inducing state of fatigue itself. Thus as the sleeper becomes more and more rested, the sleep response is less and less compellingly activated or, to put it conversely, the *antithetical* response of being awake is *more and more* compellingly activated. Consequently, as recuperation from the state of fatigue progresses, it becomes increasingly likely that quite strong or intense stimulation will *succeed* in disrupting the sleep response. *Thus the Basic Tendency (i.e., the tendency to maximize vitalizing stimulation and to minimize devitalizing stimulation), while serving to maintain sleep while the body is in a state of fatigue, serves to disrupt it when that state is no longer present.*

When a hypnotist is attempting to bring about a state

leading to hypnotic sleep, he is in effect endeavoring to induce a condition which is quite similar to that which precedes a person's falling asleep naturally. For tranquillizing the subject and circumscribing his field of sensory stimulation are means of minimizing stimulation which is potentially disruptive; and suggesting that the subject is experiencing feelings of tiredness and heaviness is a means of inducing stimulation similar to that evoked by the state of physical fatigue itself.

Where sleep is induced by some sort of psychological shock – we would speak here of being in a faint – the psychodynamics are of a quite different sort. Here the "sleep" response is elicited by the sudden occurrence of *excessive* stimulation, by stimulation which is, in fact, so overwhelming that the organism is unable to cope with it. Although such fainting serves for the moment to protect the organism against the continuing impact of the stimulation, it does *not* serve to remove the source of the stimulation itself, as natural sleep serves to remove the state of fatigue. In this respect, therefore, it is a maladaptive response.

1. In connection with this Section, see the Sections, "The Basic Tendency," pp. 3-12, "The Vitalizing Effect of Stimulation Per Se," pp. 17-18, "Dreams and the BT," pp. 118-121, and "The Function of Dreaming," pp. 122-124.

DREAMS AND THE BT[1]

When someone is asleep and dreaming, as when he is awake, he will respond in conformity with the BT. Thus he will tend to respond so as to bring about – given the limitations imposed by the situation in which he finds himself – a more favorable (or less unfavorable) V-DV stimulation balance. Insofar as the stimulation he is receiving from some source – for example, in connection with a dream thought – is *devitalizing,* say, because it is emotionally distressing, he will tend to respond so as to *reduce* its impact. On the other hand, insofar as the stimulation he is receiving from some source is *vitalizing,* he will tend to respond so as to *increase* its impact.

What are the basic methods by which a dreamer who is being subjected to a devitalizing dream thought (more exactly, if more awkwardly, to the devitalizing stimulation which is correlated with some dream thought) can *reduce* the impact of that thought? *These are the same general means, I would say, as those which may be employed by him when he is coping with a devitalizing situation in the waking state, the same general means which have been previously enumerated.*[2] *In other words, the dreamer may endeavor in some way to withdraw from the thought or to exclude it or to destroy (attack) it (that is, change it so that it will be less devitalizing). Let me point out that on this view, rooted as it is in a principle (namely, the BT) which is applicable to devitalizing stimulation regardless of whether one is dreaming or not dreaming, there is no need to invoke an imaginary "censor" or an imaginary "superego"*[3] *to protect the dreamer against emotionally distressing and sleep interfering ideas.*

This view also has implications with respect to the Freudian methods by which a latent dream thought allegedly can be transformed and disguised (viz., condensation, displacement, plastic representation and secondary elaboration). For if we adopt the frame of reference I am here proposing, these four methods become merely four subordinate ways by which such a thought can be attacked or excluded or withdrawn from.[4] With regard to Freud's four-fold classification itself, I must add that insofar as it is intended, as it presumably is, to *rule out* certain transformation possibilities, I consider it to indicate a misreading of the facts.[5] For just as an untamed animal when confronting a threatening predator will seek to protect itself, if need be, by any means at its command, so too, I believe, will an unconscious (sleeping) human being when confronting a threatening dream idea.

If a latent dream thought can be transformed in an *unrestricted number* of ways, not simply in one or more of the four ways enumerated by Freud, the task of tracing back, transformation by transformation, the *meaning* of the manifest dream content becomes, of course, proportionately more difficult. To some extent for this reason, though to a greater extent for other reasons,[6] I have considerably less faith than Freud in the overall feasibility of dream interpretation. Yet there can be no doubt that, given a sufficiently representative sample, an individual's manifest dreams are significantly correlated both with his life experiences and with his so-called "personality structure."

In this connection, in fact, I would like to call attention to what I believe to be a frequently neglected, but very basic, "dream principle," namely, that *in our dream life, as in our waking life, we are less likely to be successful in coping with a formidable threat.* Thus we are less likely to be able to protect ourselves against a dream idea which is *very markedly* devitalizing, for example, one which is associated with an experience, past or prospective, which is highly distressing. Such a dream idea, other things being equal, is more likely, not only to intrude itself into our dreams, but also to break through our defensive efforts to modify it.

On the basis of this principle, we might expect that the manifest dreams of a neurotic, or of a highly distraught, individual would, on the whole, be more revealing than those of the "normal" person and we might anticipate that the manifest dreams, not to mention the hallucinations, of the psychotic – hallucinations being, in a significant sense, the psychotic's dreams while awake – would tend to be even *more* revealing. This is, indeed, just what we find.

The strong appeal of Freud's basic thesis that dreams are an expression of our unconscious wishes (desires, drives, etc.) stemmed in part from its seeming simplicity. But Freud himself soon recognized that many of our dreams are traceable to highly disquieting, even traumatic, events in our lives, that is to say, to events which we not only would *not* wish to reexperience but which we would *wish not* to reexperience. Thus he soon was required to modify his position and to attribute the genesis of our dreams both to our wishes to *have* something occur (our desires) and to our wishes *not to have* something occur (our fears). In other words, he soon had to carry water on both shoulders. I believe this revision, however, so attenuated his wish-fulfillment thesis as to deprive it of much of its original significance.

For my own part, I would say that in coping with the dream world, as in coping with the real world, we are responding, not to any "wishes," either positive or negative, nor to any special "instincts" or "needs" or "drives,"[7] but rather to the BT, that is to say, we are responding so as to maximize vitalizing stimulation and to minimize devitalizing stimulation. Nor is there any place in my view for such fictional psychical entities as egos, censors or unconscious minds, entities which, I suggest, are manifestations of our lingering animism.[8]

1. For convenience of exposition, I speak here in the Freudian language of "latent dream ideas" and "latent dream thoughts." It should be re-

membered, however, that for me there are no psychical entities, either conscious or unconscious, which might be called "ideas" or "thoughts." The only psychical entities are stimulation indicators, including the dream images which make up what Freud calls "the manifest dream content." See the Section, "Psychical Entities," pp. 95-100, and the two Sections following it.

2. See the Section, "The Basic Forms of Response," pp. 13-16.

3. See the Section, "Guilt," pp. 151-152.

4. Since the dreamer may be viewed either as excluding or as withdrawing from the latent dream elements which are *omitted* in the manifest dream content, it is appropriate that all three methods be included. These *three general* means of coping with devitalizing dream thoughts cover *all possible particular* means.

5. I believe Freud's four transformation processes *in fact, and contrary to his assumption or intention,* permit so *much* distortion that, given any particular manifest content, we can arrive at *any* dream thought. It is as if, given some whole number, we were allowed to change it to some other whole number in any or all of the following four ways: by multiplying by 4, by dividing by 3, by adding 2 and by subtracting 1. Obviously there is no whole number at which we cannot arrive by these processes. Similarly there is no end-result which Freud's four-way "guide book" on dream interpretation in fact rules out.

6. See the Sections, "The Interpretation of the Unconscious," pp. 109-113, and "Must Human Behavior Have Meaning?," pp. 125-127.

7. See the Section, "Needs, Drives and the BT," pp. 42-44.

8. See the Section, "Animism, Psychopathology and Devitalization," pp. 136-137.

THE FUNCTION OF DREAMING

It has frequently been claimed that the biological function of dreaming, that is to say, its evolutionary raison d'etre, is the preservation of sleep, for through dreaming, it is argued, the sleeper can often transform and harmlessly siphon off sleep interfering influences. It must be borne in mind, however, that the prolongation of sleep, though it may be survival *aiding* under *some* circumstances, may be survival *jeopardizing* under *other* circumstances, for example, if the sleeper is about to be attacked or must confront some other emergency. Indeed, after the sleeper is well rested, the prolongation of sleep has only *negative* survival value.

As an alternative hypothesis, though one which admittedly is quite speculative, let me suggest that the biological function of dreaming, that is to say, its usefulness from the point of view of biological survival, may be, at least in part, *its maintenance of an adequate level of neurological activity* [1] *and thus the achievement of two highly important end-results*: (1) *the prevention of possible neurological malfunctioning and* (2) *the assurance of at least a minimal degree of emergency readiness.*

That dreaming is associated with a detectable increase in neurological activity is a conclusion to which various research studies in the field of electroencephalography give strong support. Other studies point quite clearly to the conclusion that in the absence, over a period of time, of appropriate amounts and forms of sensory stimulation (particularly in the developing infant), neurological activity may be reduced to the point where neurological functioning may be significantly impaired. Is it unreasonable to suppose, therefore, that dreaming, as one form of sensory or sensory-like experience, serves to maintain a minimal level of neurological activity during sleep and thereby to protect the sleeper against neurological malfunctioning and an excessive unreadiness to cope with a possible emergency? [2]

Let me add that on this hypothesis it becomes quite understandable why dreaming is primarily a *visual* experience. When we fall asleep, we close our eyes but we do not, of course, in any comparable way, close our ears or our other sense organs. As a result, it is that part of our neurological apparatus which processes *visual* excitations which is most sharply deactivated and whose continued functioning is most seriously endangered. Thus if dreaming serves to *maintain* an adequate level of neurological activity, *visual* dreaming would clearly have *greater* survival value than any *other* form of sensory dreaming.

Though the hypothesis which I have suggested may be speculative, the Freudian contention that the biological function of dreaming is the preservation of sleep is one which I would flatly reject. For in addition to the comment noted in the first paragraph of this Section, I would point out that it confounds and confuses the causal interrelationships. As I see it, what serves to protect an organism against devitalizing influences, whether that organism is awake or asleep, dreaming or not dreaming, is the operation of the BT. Hence when such influences – say, in the form of emotionally distressing sensations or thoughts – threaten to intrude themselves upon the dreamer, it is not that the dreaming safeguards his sleep but rather that his neurophysiological apparatus, operating in accordance with the BT, leads him to minimize stimulation which is devitalizing.[3]

1. It is not being assumed here that dream images (which are nonphysical) *bring about* neurological activity (which is physical). The assumption is rather the usual one, that dream images *require the presence* of neurological activity.

2. The findings reported (e.g., by Kleitman) with respect to the negative

personality effects of dream (as against mere sleep) disruption serve to support this hypothesis.

3. In this connection, see the Section, "Sleep in Relation to the BT", p. 116.

MUST HUMAN BEHAVIOR HAVE MEANING?

One of the basic contentions of Freudian psychoanalysis is that all psychological occurrences are determined, that nothing that takes place in the "human psyche" is a matter of chance or accident, whether it be an apparently inconsequential element in a dream, a slip of speech, or a neurotic symptom; that, on the contrary, whatever occurs has an explanation, a discoverable significance or meaning, the key to which lies (except in the relatively rare instances where organicity is present) in the interplay between certain impelling "psychic forces" (i.e., certain motives, wishes, drives, etc.) and certain "counterforces" (i.e., certain defensive and other counteracting forces). It may not be amiss to say that this thesis is, indeed, the very cornerstone of Freudian psychoanalysis. Yet the underlying argument here seems to me to be confused and invalid.

That error lies in the inference: causally explicable, therefore (exceptional instances aside) psychodynamically explicable. Of course, Freud does not present his argument in so synoptic or transparent a form but the unwarranted transition from the first thesis to the second thesis is nonetheless there.

That whatever occurs in our "psychic life," in human behavior, has a *cause,* just as events in "nature" have causes, is a broadly accepted scientific principle, whether we regard it as a tautology, as a postulate or as an empirical generalization. If we proceed to state that whatever occurs in our psychic life, in human behavior, is causally *explicable,* we may not be asserting much *more* than this, for we may be adding *merely* that the causes of such occurrences are (theoretically) *discoverable.* But certainly if we proceed still further and assert that the explanation of such occurrences — and thus that their "significance or meaning" — is normally to be found in the "psychic forces" and "counterforces" which allegedly generate them, *we are moving on to a position which goes far beyond our premises.* For clearly the characteristic causes of such occurrences, granted that such occurrences must have causes, *need not at all be "psychic forces" and "counterforces," and still less the particular kinds of "psychic forces" and "counterforces" which Freud has spelled out. This is a conclusion which vastly transcends the implications of determinism.*[1]

There is a further confusion in Freud's argument. Even if it were true that virtually everything which occurs in our "psychic life" results from the interplay of "psychic forces" and "counterforces," it does *not* follow that virtually everything which occurs there must *manifest* — that is to say, must *bear the imprint of* — that interplay, which is what Freud, in his emphasis on the meaningfulness of such occurrences, often seems to assume. For A may be the cause, or a cause, of B without its being in any way *present* in B. Thus a detective knows only too well that a criminal may or *may not* leave behind any tell-tale clues as to his identity. Nor does a clue, if one is found, which points to the criminal's *identity* necessarily point to the criminal's *motives* or *wishes,* etc. And even if the clue discloses a motive or wish, etc. in *some* degree, it will not necessarily disclose it *fully.*

In virtue of these several confusions, first, with reference to the *causative role of* (conscious or unconscious) motives, wishes, drives, etc. in relation to "psychic phenomena" and, second, with reference to their *being manifested* in such phenomena, it seems to me that *those of Freudian persuasion have tended to seek and to "find" meanings in human behavior — for example, in a dream or in a slip of speech or in a neurotic symptom — where none at all may exist.*

1. Since *all* occurrences are presumed to be determined, Freud might

have argued equally validly, or rather equally invalidly, that all phenomena, psychical or non-psychical, have such psychic determinants. Freud's logic suggests not only that a deterministic view of the universe and a teleological view are *compatible* but that the former actually *entails* the latter. This, certainly, is to give an old controversy a new twist!

TELEPATHIC COMMUNICATION

The controlled experiments in the field of human telepathic communication (i.e., direct interpersonal communication other than through the recognized forms of sense perception) of which I have any knowledge have been performed under conditions which fall far short of those which would seem to me most likely to yield positive results. In general, they appear to have been conducted under highly artificial, even antiseptic, circumstances which are markedly different from those evolutionary conditions of struggle and survival in which the usefulness of telepathy would actually have been tested.

However human telepathy (if it occurs) may have evolved, I would think that the need on the part of any person (or, for that matter, on the part of any other creature) to *avail* himself of any telepathic capacity he might possess (assuming that telepathic messages can be transmitted selectively) would be greatest in situations of unusual danger. For under such circumstances the ability to communicate with one's potential rescuers without thereby alerting one's potential enemies could literally mean the difference between life and death.[1] In my judgment, therefore *this type of context offers a much more promising field for telepathic research.*[2]

Can we narrow that context somewhat further? Since in a so-called "natural" or "primitive" environment the readiness of one human being to come to the rescue of another human being usually is most evident in the maternal relationship – and a similar statement is applicable, of course, to a number of other species – I would think that we would have special justification for looking for telepathic communication here, particularly since, if it is selective (that is, if the recipients of a telepathic transmission can be appropriately limited), it would seem reasonable to assume that receptivity depends, in part at least, on a similarity in genetic constitution. In addition to the mother-to-endangered-child relationship, perhaps one might also explore the mate-to-endangered-mate relationship. I must hasten to add, however, that I am not particularly sanguine that even in such a context any scientifically persuasive evidence of human telepathy will be uncovered.

1. Of course, if someone, through the use of telepathy, had the capacity to anticipate another human being's intention to attack him, or had the capacity to thwart an intending attacker by conveying to him a misleading "message," this too would be highly advantageous to him. However, among other things, it is difficult to see — though the objection is less than fatal — what advantages so clumsy a telepathic apparatus would be to the prospective attacker.

2. Presumably human telepathy, if it occurs at all, operates through the generation, transmission and reception of some kind of radiating waves or impulses. One might hypothesize that the generation of such waves or impulses requires the presence of a highly aroused emotional state such as is activated by confrontation with extreme danger. Perhaps telepathic receptivity, on the other hand, requires a relatively quiescent emotional state, as most telepathic proponents seem tacitly to assume.

PART FIVE

ANIMISM, PSYCHOPATHOLOGY, PSYCHOTHERAPY, ETC.

ANIMISM, PSYCHOPATHOLOGY AND DEVITALIZATION

(1) The world of the infant and of the very young child is a world in which no object is completely inanimate. Everything about him is endowed with some degree of "aliveness," i.e., with some ability to act upon him or to respond to him – of course, in a greater or lesser degree in accordance with the particular "meaning" the object has acquired for him – and only very reluctantly does he come to make the usual adult distinction between living and non-living things. I am convinced [1] that *this radical change in the character of his world, from one all of whose objects are in some measure "alive" (animate) to one most of whose objects, at least in contemporary urban society, are entirely "dead" (inanimate), can have very profound and far-reaching developmental consequences, consequences to which the psychological literature, however, has so far given but scant attention.*

(2) Freud attached considerable importance to the matter of "weaning." He indicated that faulty weaning – that is, weaning which is premature or belated or unduly harsh – in relation to a "pregenital" child's "oral" or "anal" gratifications can grossly distort the maturational process. It is my judgment that although his strictures were sound, his focus was much to narrow, that *the pregenital child must be properly weaned, not only in regard to his oral and anal gratifications, but in regard to various other gratifications as well, among them, his intense gratification in perceiving, and in relating to, the objects about him as to some extent animate. In fact I see improper animistic weaning as contributing no less significantly to the development of in-*

dividual psychopathology (at least in contemporary urban society) than improper oral or anal weaning.

(3) Thus I believe that if the transition from a world which is fully "alive" (animate) to one which is largely "dead" (inanimate) is made improperly, a child may feel himself to be separated and estranged from his new world – indeed that *in some instances the removal of his animate world may be so traumatizing (devitalizing) and the resulting sense of depersonalization or alienation so marked as to initiate the development of a schizophrenic pattern of adjustment.*[2]

(4) With respect to the schizophrenic patient himself, I would like to suggest that not infrequently the mysterious (sensory or other) "influences" with which he may believe he is in contact – influences by which he usually feels either victimized (i.e., controlled, poisoned, etc.) or especially empowered (as when he feels Christ-like or Napoleonic, etc.) – represent the reactivation of some of the "forces" (i.e., response tendencies) which formerly impelled him to *animate* his world. In other words, *they not infrequently represent the pathological emergence of his repressed animism.* (In terms of the Basic Tendency, they may be said to manifest the individual's tendency to move in the direction of a vitalizing interaction.) The situation psychodynamically is somewhat similar, I would say, where the *neurotic* individual – e.g., the phobic or highly suspicious patient – feels that mysterious "influences" are operating on or through him. The essential difference is that here the breakthrough is relatively limited, so that the "influences" are felt to be less potent and do not acquire a well-defined sensory (hallucinatory) form.

(5) My animistic thesis also has relevance with respect to adolescent or adult difficulties concerning *giving,* difficulties which, I would say, often are related not so much

to the influence of *anality* as to the influence of *animism*. Because of the young child's compelling tendency to *animate*, and hence to project something of *himself* upon, the objects which surround him, he is apt to perceive those objects, particularly those with which he is most familiar, as being not only *like* himself but a *part* of himself. *Thus to be separated from those objects is in effect to be separated from himself.* (Perhaps this "self-extension" is also a factor in relation to behavior which is claimed by some to manifest the so-called "territorial imperative." See the Section, "The Territorial Imperative," pp. 45-47.) Where this self-projecting tendency is markedly over-indulged and/or where it is terminated prematurely or harshly, it should not be surprising, therefore, that the individual's resistance to parting with objects, or to giving of himself "emotionally" or "psychologically," may reach pathological proportions.

(6) Improper animistic weaning may also, in my opinion, contribute toward bringing about an excessive fear of death or "thanatophobia." *For when a child is compelled to accept a "realistic" attitude toward a for-him-animate object* (e.g., a rattle or a doll or a train or a clock), *that object to some extent "dies"; and this experience may in turn arouse the fear that his parents or other persons (or creatures) around him, including himself, may also die.* If the weaning is in any way traumatizing, therefore, an excessive fear of death may be created.

(7) Related to the developmental sequences mentioned in numbered paragraphs (3) and (6), yet having a somewhat different psychogenesis, is the symptom of pathological depression. Where improper animistic weaning leads to pathological depression, it does so by creating a deep sense of alienation combined not with a fear of death, but with its passive anticipation. Freud recognized that pathological depression in an adult is often related to the loss of a contemporary "love object." But I would

point out that *behind the loss of that object, or even of the parental love object of which, for Freud, the contemporary object may be a surrogate, there is the earlier, and greater, loss, the "death," of almost his entire animate world. Where this loss creates a deep feeling of alienation combined with a deep sense of resignation, I believe it can trigger the development of pathological depression.*

(8) It seems quite evident that the need (tendency) for Man to live among things which are perceived as living is a very persistent and compelling one. We have merely to note the fact that it is only in the more recent moments of his history that, largely under the pressure of science, he has in any significant measure relinquished his animism. For thousands of years Man transformed the inanimate into the animate – as the child and as contemporary "primitive" Man still does.

(9) *Behind this animistic need (tendency), I suggest, is the broader need (tendency) to respond so as to be, and to feel, vitalized – to maximize stimulation which has a vitalizing effect and to minimize stimulation which has a devitalizing effect – in other words, the Basic Tendency. Just as the hunger for food is likely to lead one to perceive food-objects in a Rorschach ink-blot, so, I would suggest, does the "hunger" for other living things lead one to perceive inanimate objects as animate. In both cases, the perception of the object in this distorted way makes the object, or rather the stimulation associated with the perception of the object, more vitalizing or less devitalizing.*

(10) Man's need (tendency) to animate the inanimate has manifested itself in the course of history in at least three major areas – in his conceptualization of the world (i.e., his philosophy, his science and his religion), in his language and in his art. Natural events have been "explained" in terms of "spirits" or "forces" or "gods" of one sort or

another from time immemorial and today, even in professional circles, it is not passé to speak solemnly of such mystical and transcendental entities as egos and superegos and of minds and psychic forces. The languages of Man bear vivid testimony to his animistic conceptualizations – most obviously, perhaps, in his sexualization of objects by making them "masculine" or "feminine." So too does his art. For whether he was decorating an arrow flinthead or painting a bison on the wall of his cave, Man was projecting something of himself on to an inanimate canvas and thereby animating both the canvas and himself.[3]

(11) A review of Man's mythological and historical past reveals that certain natural but inanimate entities have been elevated almost universally into objects of worship – entities such as the sun, the moon, the rain, the wind, water, fire, etc. This has doubtless been so because of their recognized or presumed ability to affect his life drastically for good or for ill – and independently of his own wishes. It is understandable, therefore, that they should be felt to be not only supremely powerful but supremely alive. It is also understandable that Man should feel a compelling need to influence them in his behalf. Utilizing the techniques of sacrifice, of penitence, of ritual and of prayer, institutional religion has proclaimed its ability to offer Man effective ways of achieving this goal and has promised the "faithful" not only survival but, significantly, life eternal.

(12) Because Man is usually compelled in contemporary society to live among objects the vast majority of which are, and are perceived by him to be, non-living, he inevitably experiences a marked degree of frustration and insecurity. And in an effort to minimize these consequences, he resorts to a wide range of ingenious behavior patterns. Though some of these – for example, decorating frigid looking office buildings with pathetically lonely plants, having a dog at the end of every leash and commuting daily to the ever

receding suburbs — are quite innocuous, others are not. For *the responses also include socially destructive, if momentarily revitalizing, acts of delinquency, of crime and of war.*

(13) In contrast to the "existential insecurity" pointed up by the Existentialist, we might call the type of insecurity just referred to (numbered paragraph 12), "vitalistic insecurity." *Vitalistic insecurity has been brought about primarily by Man's acceptance of the scientific distinction between the animate and the inanimate and by his growing urbanization, which forces him to live among objects almost all of which are, and are perceived by him to be, inanimate.* (The major exceptions in an otherwise lifeless city landscape are people, pets, pigeons and an occasional tree — and even the people often come to be perceived as inanimate moving objects rather than as vibrant human beings!) Probably other factors too — though I would consider these to be secondary — have contributed to vitalistic insecurity. Thus in certain respects — and various writers have repeatedly emphasized this point — contemporary Man is being deindividualized, routinized and robotized. At the same time, he is being subjected to such excessive stimulation that he often feels overwhelmed and disorganized by his urban environment.

(14) The impact of urban society, however, is by no means *wholly* on the side of devitalization. For the increase in the amount and diversity of the stimulation to which city dwellers are exposed can, up to a point of overstimulation, have a very vitalizing effect.[4] Indeed, it is largely the *expectation* of such vitalization which has been impelling rural and small town dwellers in ever increasing numbers to become city dwellers. But a counter movement, at least toward suburban living, has also been under way and I would suspect that in a vast number of these instances, an uncomfortable sense of urban-induced devitalization — in effect, vitalistic insecurity — has served to bring this about.

1. The psychological conclusions presented in this Section, particularly those relating to the development of the individual (numbered paragraphs 1 through 7), are to a considerable extent rooted in my professional experience — as a practicing psychotherapist, as the Director of a mental health service and as the Director of a training institute for psychotherapists and psychoanalysts. In addition, they seem to me to have, despite their novelty, a high degree of *prima facie* plausibility. But because of limitations of space no effort is made here to substantiate those conclusions by reference to specific case histories.

2. It is generally agreed that the human being has a need for (that is, requires for his well-being) an adequate degree of responsive contact, of vitalizing interaction. The existence and potency of this need is substantiated to a greater or lesser extent not only by everyday observation but also by clinical studies ranging from those dealing with the infant's need for appropriate mothering to those relating to the confined prisoner's need for some form of interpersonal relationship. When this need is improperly met, the individual deteriorates — in my terminology, he is devitalized — and in extreme instances he may become psychotic. Can we suppose that replacing most of the live or animate (responsive) objects in a child's world with objects which are dead or inanimate (unresponsive) may not at times have comparable effects?

3. See the Section, "Creation, Animism and the BT," p. 197.

4. See the Section, "The Vitalizing Effect of Stimulation Per Se," pp. 17-18. For a discussion of overstimulation in relation to social change, see Alvin Toffler's *Future Shock* (Random House, 1970).

SOME MISCELLANEOUS VITALIZATION PATTERNS

Numerous are the ways – I am speaking here of relatively *particular* response patterns falling within the overall, or "basic," forms of response[1] – in which Man vitalizes himself, that is to say, in which he maximizes his contact with sources of vitalizing stimulation and minimizes his contact with sources of devitalizing stimulation. In the preceding Section, attention was called to some reaction patterns which are activated by the inanimate character of his environment; in other Sections, reaction patterns activated in other contexts have been noted. Here let me mention various *interests, values and attitudes* which betray Man's tendency to vitalize himself or, to put it differently, which betray the operation of the BT. These are consequences of the fact that, other things being equal, what is perceived as "alive" or as "vital" is apt to be vitalizing and hence pleasing and maximized[2] – or of the converse fact that what is perceived as "dead" or "lifeless" is apt to be devitalizing and hence displeasing and minimized. I would mention, for example:

(1) the increasing interest, among persons who are in their declining years, in returning (in reality or in fantasy) to the vitalizing stimuli associated with their childhood;[3]

(2) the sense of refreshment we feel in observing the spontaneity and directness of the responses of the young;

(3) our pleasure in perceiving that which is new or fresh or clean;

(4) the extent to which we give our attention to that

member of a group who strikes us as being the most "dynamic" (alive);

(5) our readiness to admire that which seems vigorous or strong;

(6) our negative reaction to what impresses us as being non-natural or artificial or repetitious or predictable or constricted or rigid – in brief, to what impresses us as being uncharacteristic of what is vital;

(7) our sense of repugnance, even horror, when perceiving various forms of decay or injury or malformation or destruction;[4]

(8) our feeling of discomfort in the absence of any kind of change or variety or movement;[5]

(9) our general resistance to any kind of externally imposed controls;

(10) the emphasis, in virtually all societies, on the value of freedom, that is, on the value of freedom *for* the society if not on its value *within* the society.

1. See the Section, "The Basic Forms of Response," pp. 13-16.

2. See the Sections, "A Related Principle Concerning Affect," pp. 19-20, and "Animism, Psychopathology and Devitalization," p. 136.

3. It may be speculated that the return of the salmon, and certain other species, to the place of their birth is similarly impelled.

4. Castration anxiety is doubtless only one, albeit psychodynamically a relatively important, example of this type of reaction.

5. In this connection, let me mention our persistent need (tendency) to refocus our sensory apparatus. Thus when a person follows a moving object with his eyes, his eye movements are jerky rather than continuous; and when he stares for several seconds at any fixed object, he soon breaks the monotony by shifting his glance elsewhere. Since the vitalizing (and attention-getting) impact of any new sensory stimulus, be it through sight or touch or smell, etc., tends to diminish, the refocusing of that sensory apparatus has the effect of recapturing that impact.

SELF-DESTRUCTIVE BEHAVIOR

A positive response to vitalizing stimulation or a negative response to devitalizing stimulation tends to increase or maintain the vitalization level of an organism and hence to achieve its preservation or survival. But it does not *guarantee* its preservation or survival and in the course of such behavior, or as a by-product of such behavior, an organism may suffer injury or death.

Thus an animal responding positively to a momentarily vitalizing drink *may* be absorbing a death-dealing poison; or one which is escaping from a frightening fire *may* be drowned; or a child who persists in demanding attention *may* receive a spanking; or an adult attracted by the excitement of driving his car at break-neck speed *may* be killed. Behavior which is in accord with the BT, whether it is unlearned or learned, though it *tends* to make for the preservation (the survival) of the organism, does not *assure* it, and in some instances the response may bring about, directly or as an eventual consequence, the injury or destruction of the organism.

Does this fact, however, point to the existence of a self-destructive "need" or "drive" or "instinct"? In my judgment, it does not. In my view, *the resultant self-destruction is simply a by-product or end-result of the operation of the BT.*

Of course, one individual may have a greater tendency than another to act in a way which is likely to prove self-destructive. This may be so in virtue of any one of a variety of factors. Thus one person may be less agile or less discerning or more adventurous than another. Or it may be that for one person the prospect of danger, being relatively more vitalizing, is more action-impelling (less action-inhibiting). But here too the behavior is in conformity with the Basic Tendency; and the hypothesis that it is the product of a self-destructive "need" or "drive" or "instinct" is, I believe, neither necessary nor demonstrable.

To be sure, if we were to inquire into the "motives" of human beings, we would find some people saying that in certain situations they ("consciously" or "unconsciously") *wanted* to injure or destroy themselves. And of course some people *do* injure or destroy themselves, whether by involving themselves in self-defeating activities of one sort or another or by resorting to outright mutilation or suicide. But the fundamental dynamic factor here is the BT, not the alleged intention or wish. For the person who says or feels that he wants to injure or destroy himself, and in fact does so, is nonetheless responding in accordance with the BT, that is to say, he is responding (given the absence of organically or traumatically induced pathology) so as to maintain or improve his present V-DV stimulation balance, and the self-destruction is merely a by-product or secondary consequence of this fact, albeit one which, in a sense, he may have sought. *Just as Man's desire or ability to ascend into the stratosphere in no way abrogates or nullifies the operation of the law of gravitation, so too his desire or ability to destroy himself in no way abrogates or nullifies the operation of the BT.*

MASOCHISM OR COUNTERACTION?

When I have found myself in a situation in which I anticipated being subjected to a momentary physical pain — for example, when a physician has been about to insert a hypodermic needle in my arm — I have noticed that I have sometimes pressed one of my fingernails into my flesh, apparently to "counteract" the anticipated pain. I would like to suggest that this way of dealing with a painful or unpleasant situation is much more extensively employed than has been generally recognized and that *many forms of behavior, among them, many which have been labeled "masochistic" or "self-punitive" or even "self-destructive," can be regarded as manifestations of "counteraction." It should be added that the counteractive response is in accord with the BT; it is one way of responding so as to reduce the impact of devitalizing stimulation.*

How many forms of behavior can be regarded as "counteractive" depends, of course, on how narrowly or broadly we define the term. Although we can limit the term so that it covers (as in the instance cited) only the *deliberate* imposition of a *somatically* induced *pain* for the *conscious* purpose of offsetting some other *somatically* induced *pain,* any such restricted use of the term would seem to be highly arbitrary. For the same mechanism appears to be at work in situations which do *not* involve the italicized limitations — say, for example, when an individual endures a very mild degree of psychological discomfort by remaining at the bedside of a sick friend, seemingly in order to avoid or reduce his guilt feelings. To encompass *all* the situations in which the same mechanism appears to be operative, I would therefore define "counteraction" as *any* sufferance of any somatically or *psychologically* induced pain or *discomfort* for the presumed purpose, conscious or *unconscious,* of offsetting some other somatically or *psychologically* induced pain or *discomfort.*

The mechanism of "counteraction," as the term is here used, not only has very wide *practical application* but seems to me to be of considerable *theoretical importance,* bringing together under one roof, so to speak, many forms of behavior whose underlying identity has heretofore not been clearly perceived.

Thus, for example, it includes the suffering-first-to-have-pleasure-later form of response as well as the suffering-later-where-one-has-had-pleasure-first form of response, since in either case we can consider the suffering to be a way of warding off – of counteracting – an *anticipated* suffering.

It has sometimes been contended that there are forms of masochism in which pain is sought *in and for itself* or at least for the pleasure which the pain itself presumably elicits. In regard to this contention, I would like to note first that *if* it is true in a given instance that, in a certain sense, pain is being sought *in and for itself,* it cannot (i.e., without self-contradiction) *also* be true that, in that sense, pain is being sought for some *other* end or purpose, viz., for pleasure. But I would also like to point out that if, in a given instance and in a certain sense, pain is being sought *either* in and for itself *or* for the pleasure it presumably elicits, the presence of such a motive is fully reconcilable with the operation of the BT. For *the logic of the situation is clearly the same whether we are talking, as in the preceding Section, about a motive to injure or destroy oneself or, as in this Section, about a motive to experience pain.* In either case, the presence of a motive, or the ability to carry it out, in no way abrogates or nullifies the fact that, given the absence of organically or traumatically induced pathology, one is responding to a stimulus situation so as to maintain or improve the present V-DV stimulation balance.[1]

REFLECTIONS

1. See the final paragraph of the preceding Section, "Self-Destructive Behavior."

THE DEFENSE MECHANISMS

Given the theoretical framework provided by the Basic Tendency, *a psychological defense mechanism* (projection, denial, repression, rationalization, counteraction, etc.) *may be viewed as a means of reducing the devitalizing stimulation elicited by a given source without having recourse to any overt physical action, at least in relation to the source itself*. Here there is no physical attack upon a devitalizing source nor any physical escape from it nor any physical exclusion of it. For here it is primarily something *subjective* – e.g., a "feeling" or an "idea" which is attacked or withdrawn from or excluded.[1] And this is accomplished by resorting to a kind of now-you-see-it-now-you-don't intracranial trick, more specifically, by blocking or re-routing or otherwise modifying certain neurological impulses.

A defensive response of this sort, in contrast to an overt physical action response, is thus, in a sense, an unrealistic, even a self-deceptive, way of coping with devitalizing stimulation. For neither the external cause itself (e.g., the hypodermic needle jabbing one's arm or one's poor performance in a certain situation) nor one's physical relationship to that external cause is in any way changed by it. However, we must remember that in many instances remedial responses toward the devitalizing source on the level of overt physical action are, in the nature of the case, unavailable to us, as, for example, in dealing with an upsetting situation which is completely past or in dealing with a current and continuing situation (as when one is confronting a fatal illness) which cannot be effectively altered and from which we cannot physically extricate ourselves.

Let me add a remark of a more speculative nature. A

defense mechanism is a form of response which presumably has come to be available to Man (and to certain other species) in virtue of its usefulness in relation to survival. But because, as noted above, it is, in a sense, an *unrealistic* adjustive mechanism, its employment, particularly in connection with a genuinely dangerous situation, can be grossly self-defeating. I would suggest that, faced as the human race currently is with the paralyzing possibility of complete extermination, it may well be Man's capacity to resort to defense mechanisms which will prove to be his Achilles' heel.[2]

1. See the Sections, "The Basic Forms of Response," pp. 13-16, and "Dreams and the BT," pp. 118-121.
2. See the Section, "International Insanity," pp. 192-193.

PSYCHOSOMATIC SYMPTOMS

It is commonly held in medical and psychological circles that much of Man's physical illness is "psychosomatic," that is to say, that a wide range of pathological changes in his body functioning, changes which may themselves in some instances result in structural pathology, may be brought about by the (acute or chronic) presence of some negative feeling or emotion, a feeling or emotion such as anxiety, fear, worry, depression, hostility, anger, etc.

The essential truth of the thesis which is being asserted here is no longer a matter of dispute. But I would suggest that because of the confusing way (which I myself have intentionally followed here) in which that thesis characteristically is formulated – specifically, because of the causative role which it assigns to feelings or emotions – *a number of persons have been misled into drawing philosophical conclusions regarding the impact of "the mental upon the physical" or of "the mind upon the body" which are quite unwarranted.*

The basic facts, I would say, are simply these. When any feeling or emotion, negative or positive, emerges, there are concomitant changes, in certain respects, in one's body functioning, for example, in one's pulse rate, one's respiratory rate, the nature and extent of one's glandular secretions, one's muscular tensions, etc. And *it is these changes in body functioning which may bring about psychosomatic symptomatology, not the affect itself, that is, not the stimulation indicator, which is psychical.* (In other words, it is these changes in body functioning on which the symptoms are "ontologically dependent.")[1]

That there should be a higher correlation between *negative* feelings and emotions and the development of pathology is not at all surprising. For the presence of *negative* affect, unlike *positive* affect, normally indicates that the individual is being subjected to stimulation which is, in some respect, devitalizing and hence that the functional efficiency of his body is, in some respect, being reduced.[2] Understandably, therefore, where negative affect has been present over an extended period of time, or in an acute form, somatic "symptoms" are quite apt to occur.[3]

1. See the Section, "Psychophysical Interactionism," pp. 62-64.

2. See the Section, "A Related Principle Concerning Affect," pp. 19-20. As previously noted, a stimulus situation (say, one inducing anger) which is devitalizing in *some* respect may be vitalizing in some *other* respect. See the Sections, "The Basic Tendency," p. 10, and "The Basic Forms of Response," p. 16.

3. Such symptoms may be induced relatively *directly* or relatively *indirectly*. They are induced *indirectly* when the devitalization merely brings about a reduction in the body's *resistance* to some symptom-inducing factor.

GUILT

The presence of a feeling of guilt normally involves the presence of a conflict, a conflict between what one believes one *has* done (or felt, or thought, etc.) and what one believes one *ought* to have done (or felt, or thought, etc.) instead.[1] Implicit is the belief, I would say the *irrational* belief, that one *need* not have acted as one *did* act, that one had, in an indeterministic sense, a "freedom of choice."[2] Sometimes, however, a feeling of guilt, like a feeling of anxiety, is more or less "free floating," that is to say, is not related by the individual to any *specific* act or acts of his. Where the feeling of guilt is free floating, or where, either quantitatively or otherwise, it is considered to be *inappropriately* related to the act in question, a therapist may speak of it as "neurotic" rather than as "normal" guilt.

Consistent with the tendency among contemporary therapists to accept a system of values oriented toward self-gratification is the inclination in some quarters to consider virtually *any* feeling of guilt, whether "neurotic" or "normal," as a superfluous psychological entity which in fact it is better for us never to experience. But just as a feeling of pain, however, undesirable it may be in and of itself, can serve a desirable end – more specifically, can serve a *corrective* function in relation to behavior – so too, certainly, can a feeling of guilt.[3]

The notion that a feeling of guilt is brought about by, or is in any other way related to, a "superego," in the sense of an internal psychical agent of some kind, is one which, by implication at least, I have already rejected. In my view the inhibition (rejection) of a potentially guilt-provoking response is brought about, not by the operation of any such fictitious "superego," but (as in the case, e.g., of a potentially *pain*-producing response) *by the devitalizing stimulation which is elicited by the anticipation, or by the incipient activation, of that response. In other words, the devitalizing stimulation is minimized, in accordance with the BT, by not carrying out the response.*

1. In regard to "conflict," see the Section, "The Psychogenesis of Psychopathology," pp. 161-163.

2. See the Section, "Free Will and Free Choice," pp. 69-70.

3. The causally instrumental factor here — that is, the factor on which the corrective response is ontologically dependent — is not the subjective component of the feeling (that is, not the stimulation indicator) but certain neurophysiological correlates.

MAN'S INNATE NATURE

One of the questions with which classical and medieval philosophers often concerned themselves was: What is the *natural* motion of physical objects? In other words, in what way are physical objects inclined to move *in and of themselves,* that is, apart from any influence by, or relationship to, anything else? Is their "natural" motion upward or downward, in a straight line or in a curved line, at a steady or at an accelerated rate, etc.? Ingenious arguments, largely teleological or theological, were presented in support of the various conclusions which were reached.

Should we re-examine this question today in terms of its logical structure, I believe we would see at once that it is a theoretically unanswerable and hence absurd question for the reason that it presupposes the possible existence of a logically (not merely physically) impossible situation, namely, one in which a physical object may move without relationship to anything else — in other words, for the reason that it presupposes the possible occurrence of absolute motion. Yet I would like to point out that *a logically similar question, one relating to the nature of Man, is still being very seriously debated in certain circles today.* I am referring to the question: Is Man innately evil or innately good? Innately hostile or innately loving? Innately aggressive or innately unaggressive? *If what is being asked here is: "In what way would Man behave if he were free of any influence by, or relationship to, his environment?," I would suggest that we are raising a question which is no less absurd than that which was asked in regard to the natural motion of physical objects — and for exactly the same reason, namely, the presupposition of a logically impossible situation.*

Admittedly, however, questions about Man's innate nature may *not* be of this order. Thus what we *may* be asking, if only implicitly, is some question about his inherent propensity to behave in a certain way *given the presence of developmental and other environmental conditions of a certain kind, for example, conditions which are reasonably "representative" or "typical."* It is *this* general frame of reference which is presupposed in the following Section.

MAN'S AGGRESSIVENESS AND MAN'S FUTURE

Much has been written about Man's innate (or instinctual)[1] aggressiveness, that is to say, about his inherent (genetically rooted) propensity, given developmental and other environmental conditions which are reasonably "representative" or "typical," to be ruthlessly self-assertive and, not infrequently, callously destructive. Perhaps it is Freud in particular who has given currency to this thesis, a thesis which is regarded by many, if not as dooming Man to extinction, then at least as condemning him to a state of unrelenting strife and warfare.[2]

Without undertaking anything approaching a full analysis of this thesis — which would require, among other things, a more rigorous definition of terms — let me briefly set forth some of the bio-psychological considerations which lie "on the other side."

(1) One of these, of course, is that however much Man's disposition to behave aggressively may be a function of (i.e., may be affected by) his genetic constitution, it is also a function of the developmental and other environmental influences to which he happens to be subjected. Thus by appropriately altering the character of his environment, by methods ranging from parent education to the administration of drugs, we should be able, if we wish to do so, to *curtail* his aggressive behavior.

(2) Moreover Man's genetic constitution is *itself* in some degree modifiable, not only *indirectly* through the use of breeding techniques, but also *directly* — for example, by infusing the chromosomal material with certain chemical agents or by subjecting that material to radioactive bombardment.

Admittedly, however, we have not yet arrived at the point where we can *directly* alter Man's genetic constitution in a manner which is precisely predictable or even in a manner which is predictably positive.

(3) Writers who have taken the position that Man's innate (or instinctual) aggressiveness condemns him to a future "black with strife and struggle" often seem to hold that there is some kind of non-physical dynamism or propelling force operating within him which somehow *compels* him to act aggressively. Thus they are inclined to see Man as a helpless victim, so to speak, of his own pugnatious psyche. But as I have already indicated,[3] such a hypothesis transcends the observable data, is without any explanatory value and, in the light of the Basic Tendency, is entirely gratuitous.

(4) Finally let me call attention to the fact, often overlooked, that an aggressive response, at least when it becomes an attacking or destroying response,[4] *is not a primary but a secondary response,* that is, one which normally is made only when a positive type of response cannot achieve the same end, more specifically, the same level of vitalization. Thus, for example, if a human infant cannot have something he wants, he will then but only then resort to a temper tantrum and seek to injure or destroy. Indeed it would seem that given even a *moderately* favorable developmental environment, an infant's orientation toward his world is apt to become increasingly outgoing and increasingly *positive.*[5]

Though the several considerations which have been noted here may not provide a basis for unmitigated *optimism* in regard to Man's future, they undoubtedly *do* point up the fact that human nature is at least not *unalterably* perverse, if indeed it is perverse at all. Moreover, we must remember that the destiny of Man will be determined not merely by broad *bio-psychological* factors such as the degree of his "aggressiveness" but by a vast number of *other* ingredients, including demographic, ecological, technological and political factors, as well.[6]

1. The term "instinctual" is usually used in a somewhat narrower sense than the term "innate." For one thing, it is more apt to involve a reference, expressed or implied, to the adaptive (survival) value of the behavior in question.

2. Much more recently, Konrad Lorenz in *On Aggression,* Robert Ardrey in *The Territorial Imperative* and Anthony Storr in *Human Aggression* have taken a very similar position.

3. See the Sections, "The Basic Tendency Versus Other Life-Principles," pp. 22-26, "Instinct and the BT," pp. 34-41, "Needs, Drives and the BT," pp. 42-44, and "Self-Destructive Behavior," pp. 142-143.

4. See the Section, "The Basic Forms of Response," pp. 13-16.

5. I would suggest that the fact that the attacking or destroying response is a secondary response is related to the fact that, being a negative response which in its initial phase is a positive response, it is a relatively *complex* response and thus one which would develop relatively slowly.

6. See the Sections, "The Defense Mechanisms," pp. 147-148, and "International Insanity," pp. 192-193.

REWARD THEORY, VITALIZATION AND CONDITIONING

Some exponents of a reward theory of learning seem to take the position that the significant events in relation to learning occur in this sequence, namely, that a *stimulus* or *cue* elicits a *response,* that this *response* leads to a *reward* (or non-reward) – conceived either as something which gratifies (or frustrates) the organism, or as the resultant state of gratification (or frustration) itself – and that this *reward* (or non-reward) *then strengthens* (or weakens) *the connection between that type of response and that type of stimulus or cue.* In this view, a reward possesses, in effect, a "stamping in" power and a non-reward, a "stamping out" power.

As I see it, however, this is not at all the case; a reward, regardless of how it may be conceived, does *not* have any power to "stamp in" any response-to-stimulus connection nor a non-reward any power to "stamp out" any response-to-stimulus connection. Indeed, the assumption which seems to be implicit here, namely, that a reward or non-reward can operate *retroactively* is, I would say, quite absurd.

To be sure, it is possible to state a reward theory of learning in a manner which apparently, at least, avoids this difficulty. But even so it is a theory which in my judgment is open to objection. For as I see it, one learns to do something, not because it has been rewarded – *a view which makes the reward a unique and mysterious causal agent which alone possesses the power in some magical way to bring about the learning* – but because doing it maximizes vitalizing stimulation or minimizes devitalizing stimulation, i.e., is in accord with the Basic Tendency. Thus if a hungry animal is consistently given food after it performs a stunt correctly and is consistently denied food after it performs a stunt incorrectly, *it is not that the reward (conceived either as the food or as the resulting gastronomical state) somehow "strengthens" or "reinforces" the correct response; it is rather that the stimulation elicited by the correct performance becomes, through conditioning, increasingly vitalizing and hence increasingly maximized and that the stimulation elicited by the incorrect performance becomes, through conditioning, increasingly devitalizing and hence increasingly minimized.*[1]

Conditioning is possible, of course, in virtue of the "association" of one stimulation source with another, more specifically, in virtue of the linking or fusion of their neurologically induced impulses. Thus a stimulation source which initially gave rise to one form of response – say, a weak moving away response – may come to give rise to a different, even an "opposite," form of response – say, a vigorous moving toward response. In other words, a stimulation source eliciting devitalizing stimulation may, through conditioning, come to elicit vitalizing stimulation and vice versa.[2]

1. The increasingly vitalizing stimulation is increasingly *maximized,* of course, *by performing the correct response increasingly* and the increasingly devitalizing stimulation is increasingly *minimized by avoiding the incorrect response increasingly.*

2. Other things being equal, the stronger the V or DV stimulation induced by the unconditioned stimulation source, the greater is its positive or negative conditioning effect. The effect may or may not be increased, however, by extending (i.e., continuing or repeating) the presentation of the stimulation source. Whether we are considering an advertisement, a political speech, a paternal threat or an electric shock, impact may be lost by continued or repeated presentation as well as gained.

THE GENESIS OF PSYCHOPATHOLOGY

I would like to set forth in broad outline my view in regard to the genesis of psychopathology or, more precisely, the genesis of behavior which is likely to be considered to be psychopathological by the qualified professional. I shall be focusing on the *basic ways* in which psychopathology is generated rather than on the *developmental process itself.*[1] And I shall be excluding from consideration psychopathology which is *organically* generated, which is brought about, for example, by constitutional defect or by surgery or by accident or injury or by the ingestion of drugs or by the alteration of the external physical conditions affecting the organism. This leaves us, I would say, with two, and only two, other basic ways in which psychopathology may be induced. These are (a) through faulty learning and/or (b) through what I call, using the term in a somewhat special sense, "traumatization."

(a) It seems clear that a wide variety of response patterns which may be considered psychopathological can be acquired simply through the "misapplication" of the normal processes of learning, that like a computer, a person may come to make the "wrong" response simply because he has been fed the "wrong" data and that no internal malfunctioning on the part of the computer or organism need be present. Thus if a "normal" child were programmed in certain "abnormal" ways, he would learn to lie down when he is told to sit, to place his right hand over his right ear when he yawns, to despise all persons with red hair and to be strongly aroused sexually when he sees his mother. In brief, a broad spectrum of so-called psychopathological response patterns can be learned by the human being in just this way, behavior patterns ranging from the sub-normal and the immature on the one hand to the anti-social and the bizarre on the other hand. It should be added that although traumatizing situations need not have played a role in *generating* such behavior, an individual whose deviant conduct elicits the marked disapproval of his society is more likely, in *consequence* of that disapproval, to be *subjected* to traumatization.[2] Let me now turn to traumatization as a source of psychopathology.

(b) As indicated in various other Sections relating to the BT, an organism tends to make a negative (minimizing) response to stimulation which is devitalizing. However, stimulus situations can give rise, suddenly or accumulatively (i.e., in consequence of a summation of influences operating over a more or less extended period of time), to such an overwhelming degree of devitalizing stimulation that, momentarily at least, the organism is to some extent "traumatized".[3] By this I mean that it is unable (either through overt physical action or through the use of a "defense mechanism")[4] to make a response which effectively reduces the devitalizing stimulation, with the result that certain of its responses become more or less blocked, exaggerated or chaotic, perhaps to such a degree as to be labeled "psychopathological." Physiologically, traumatization – whether induced by an exploding bomb, by harsh weaning or by persistent emotional rejection – is brought about (in the more "advanced" species of organisms) by the disruption of some of the afferent-efferent neural pathways or interconnections.[5]

From the psychodynamic point of view, *traumatization occurs when a compelling (i.e., very strongly activated) positive or negative response tendency in relation to some stimulus situation is excessively thwarted.* Traumatization thus involves conflict, conflict between the compelling response tendency, on the one hand, and the (devitalizing) stimulus situation making for excessive thwarting, on the other. In human beings, but probably not only in human beings, such thwarting situations may include culturally internalized restraints (prohibitions), popularly one's "conscience" or "sense of guilt." The excessive thwarting does not always result, however, as in the case of guilt, from the activation of some incompatible response tendency; it may also be brought about by the physical situation itself.[6]

With regard to the compelling positive or negative response tendency which is thwarted, it should be noted that no limitation is specified as to its *nature,* only as to its strength. Thus it may be a response tendency which would be characterized as sexual or as aggressive or, in contrast to the Freudian view, in some *other* way. Suppose, for example, one is fleeing from a source of danger and, in the course of flight, accidentally becomes physically disabled so that one cannot continue; a state of panic may ensue which, if prolonged, may be followed by very considerable psychopathology. Unless we use the terms "sexual" and/or "aggressive" so broadly as to be virtually meaningless, there is nothing "sexual" or "aggressive" which is involved here – just the (thwarted) response tendency in the direction of escape from danger.[7] Nor is sexuality or aggression clearly involved in any of various *other* kinds of situations in which the thwarting of a compelling response tendency may elicit psychopathology, for example, where one in confronted with an unbearable degree of boredom or pain or work pressure or noise, etc. (In this connection, see the Section, "Needs, Drives and the BT," pp. 42-44, in which the concept of disparate instincts, needs or drives is rejected in favor of the BT itself.)

What has been said here in regard to psychopathology induced by traumatization can be presented synoptically as follows:

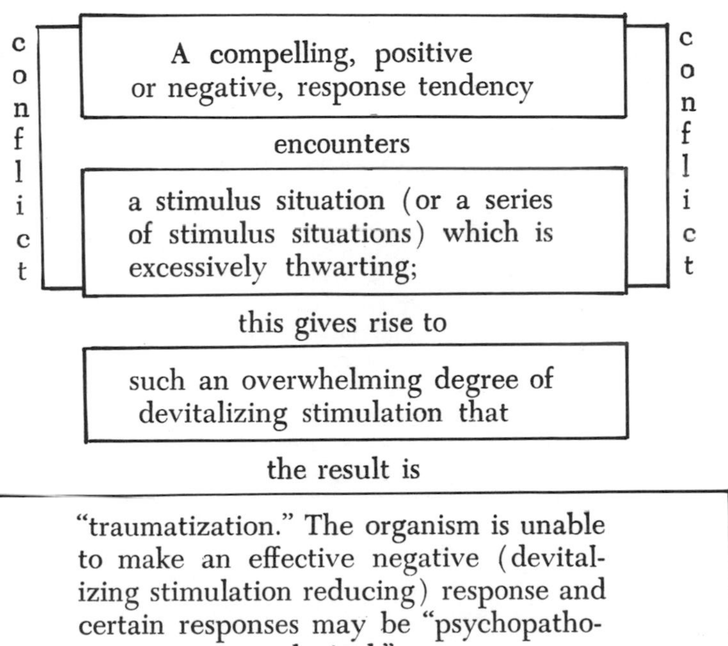

"traumatization." The organism is unable to make an effective negative (devitalizing stimulation reducing) response and certain responses may be "psychopathological."

As for the distinctive merits of the view which has been outlined here (apart from its claim to being true!), it should be pointed out that its applicability is in no way limited to *certain particular forms* of human psychopathology, for example, to the neuroses or, indeed, as the Freudian theory is,[8] to *human* psychopathology *alone*. And it is applicable not only to *naturally* induced psychopathology but to *artificially* (experimentally) induced psychopathology as well – for example, to the experimental rat which, having been *made* "neurotic," can no longer move either toward or away from either the food box or the electric shock box. It should be noted, moreover, that what is said about psychopathology induced by traumatization is rooted in the Basic Tendency, a principle which is applicable to *all* organic species and to various *levels* of response. There has been no need to explain psychopathological reactions in terms of special or restricted concepts which have been devised solely for that purpose.

1. In regard to the developmental process, see particularly the Section, "Animism, Psychopathology and Devitalization," pp. 133-136.

2. In most instances, apparently, a conventionally approved or conformist or normal response is more vitalizing than any conventionally disapproved or non-conformist or abnormal response would be, but in certain instances the reverse is true. Sometimes the mere *notion* that one is responding in a conventionally disapproved or non-conformist or abnormal way is vitalizing. This is particularly apt to be so in some forms of psychopathic (anti-social) or self-destructive or sexually deviant behavior.

3. It should be remembered (see the Section, "The Basic Tendency," p. 5) that stimulation (e.g., that induced by heat or, for that matter, by any other source) which at a certain level of intensity may be *vitalizing* to an organism and hence tend to elicit a *positive* response may at a different level of intensity be *devitalizing* to that organism and hence tend to elicit a *negative* response.

4. A "defense mechanism" (projection, denial, repression, rationalization, counteraction, etc.) is a way of reducing devitalizing stimulation without resorting to an overt physical action response toward its source. See the Section, "The Defense Mechanisms," pp. 147-148. Presumably the use of defense mechanisms is limited to Man and to other relatively "advanced" species.

5. Traumatization by one stimulus situation tends to spread, of course, to various related stimulus situations. It is in those relatively rare instances where, for one reason or another, it does *not* spread that "dramatic cures," such as those which impressed the early Freud, can be effected. *Generally speaking, psychopathology resulting from traumatization is more difficult to deal with psychotherapeutically than psychopathology resulting from faulty learning.*

6. If a compelling response tendency to run away is thwarted by "a sense of guilt," we *do* have incompatible response tendencies; if it is thwarted by physical restraint, we *do not* have incompatible response tendencies. But in both cases we have conflict, conflict, that is, between a compelling response tendency and a thwarting situation. See the Section, "The Basic Tendency," p. 10. A therapist may diminish the conflicting

impact of incompatible response tendencies by (a) reducing the degree of their divergence and/or (b) appropriately modifying their relative (or absolute) strength.

7. With respect to the stimulus situation *from* which one is seeking to escape, this is a *negative* response. With respect to the stimulus situation *toward* which one is seeking to escape, this is a *positive* response.

8. Despite Freud's background in the medical and biological sciences, his conceptual framework seems to me "all too human," all too anthropocentric. In other words, many of his major structural and developmental concepts — the tripartite self, the unconscious, repression, the censor, the Oedipus complex, castration anxiety, etc. — have little or no explanatory value in relation to the responses of *other* life forms, whatever their explanatory value may be in relation to the behavior of Man.

VITALISTIC PSYCHOTHERAPY

Having in mind some of the considerations bearing on vitalization and devitalization which are set forth in other Sections,[1] as well as certain related considerations, I should like to present a psychotherapeutic viewpoint or position which I call "Vitalistic Psychotherapy." Of necessity its exposition here will be in summary form.

The therapeutic aim of the vitalistic psychotherapist is to modify the patient's orientation toward the world so as to increase the range and depth of his vitalizing responses.[2] This requires in part that he perceive the world more "realistically," that is to say, in a manner less contaminated by devitalizing distortions (unwarranted suspicions, fears, hostilities, etc.). But it also requires (since mere validity of perception is insufficient) that the patient bring to his perception of the world a functionally more constructive perspective. This perspective can be described phenomenologically as one which to a greater degree facilitates responses characterized by a sense of creative fulfillment.

For the vitalistic therapist, such symptoms as depression, anxiety, hostility, suspiciousness, withdrawal, alienation, depersonalization, hallucinations, etc. normally indicate the presence of a stimulus situation which is in some degree devitalizing, one which therefore tends to induce some form of negative response. Though the vitalistic therapist recognizes that such life-limiting patterns of response in some instances can be dealt with directly, he believes that in the main they must be dissolved indirectly, as a by-product of personality re-vitalization. This calls for the establishment of a psychological climate (i.e., the incentives, the rewards and other stimulus conditions) in which psychological growth (vitalization) is apt to occur and for an empathic exploration, in such depth as is indicated, of the patient's thoughts, feelings, attitudes and values. Throughout this exploration the vitalistic therapist is deeply mindful of the role which the need for vitalization,[3] more specifically, which the operation of the Basic Tendency, has played and will continue to play in relation to all aspects of the patient's psychological behavior. He thus has available to him a unique tool for the understanding of that behavior.

Vitalistic therapy lays claim to no hitherto undiscovered treatment techniques but implicit in the vitalistic therapist's goal and theoretical substructure are certain quite distinctive treatment approaches and methods of procedure. Stated somewhat differently, what is distinctive in this regard is the range of the techniques he employs and when and how and why he employs them. Though directing himself toward the achievement of greater vitalization, the vitalistic therapist is keenly aware that in all human beings their vitalization potential is to a greater or lesser extent unrealized. Thus he looks upon a so-called "patient," not as falling into a sharply separate or separable psychological category, but rather as someone who, like the rest of us, is in some degree and in some respect unfulfilled.[4]

For the vitalistic psychotherapist, the kinds of psychogenic factors which can bring about less-than-optimum vitalization are numerous and varied. He rejects the marked overemphasis which he finds in certain other psychotherapeutic theories on some *particular* psychogenic factor, such as pregenital fixation, unresolved oedipal conflict, faulty identification, frustration of the power drive, basic anxiety, etc. At the same time, he believes that certain kinds of psychogenic factors which have played an important role in relation to personality maldevelopment have heretofore been almost completely neglected. Among these he would give special attention to improper animistic weaning and to the prolonged subjection of an individual to a de-animated physical environment.[5] Related to these, but less neglected, is the de-humanizing, or as I would prefer to say, devitalizing influence of contemporary Man's *cultural* environment.[6]

The vitalistic therapist rejects any treatment approach which directly or indirectly leads the patient to perceive himself — or others — as driven by certain kinds of mystical forces or other non-existent psychical entities, whether conscious or unconscious; for he believes there is no place in psychotherapeutic theory — or practice — for animistic projections, whether wicked or benign.[7] With realism yet with reverence, he conceives of the human being as an amazingly complex and variable physical mechanism which, like any other physical mechanism, has certain response possibilities[8] and "within" which, under certain circumstances, (the subjective components of) sensations and images — what I call "stimulation indicators" — occur.[9] And he recognizes that homo sapiens, like other living organisms, functions in accordance with the BT. Where indicated, the vitalistic therapist conveys his conception of the human being to the patient.

The vitalistic therapist understands that if he is to be maximally effective in vitalizing the patient, he must manifest his own sense of vitalization. For he realizes that learning in the therapeutic relationship, as, for instance, in the child-parent relationship, may occur as much through osmosis as through verbal interchange, as much through example as through precept. This is not to say, of course, that the therapist must exude a blatant optimism about life but simply that he must be, and must appropriately (quietly or otherwise) reveal himself to be, deeply in contact with his own positive feelings toward life. For only then can he also be deeply in contact with the patient.

For the vitalistic therapist, a patient's awareness of the therapist's deep contact with him is one of the major factors in the healing process. For it is frequently through this feeling of being, perhaps for the first time, profoundly in touch with another person, and therefore with himself, that the patient is enabled to respond to some heretofore rejected, or neglected, source of vitalization in a more positive manner. In other words, it is often through this means that some barrier to optimum vitalization is effectively surmounted. Indeed, for the vitalistic therapist the "depth" of the therapeutic relationship is to be measured not so much in terms of the chronological priority or even the "degree of unconsciousness" of what is explored as it is in terms of the vitalizing resonance of this sense of mutual contact.

Rigidity in any form is incompatible with optimum vitalization, whether found in the patient or in the therapist. The vitalistic psychotherapist, therefore, so far as practical and professional considerations allow, operates within a context which, though structured, is also fluid, the degree of structure and the degree of fluidity varying – again, so far as practical and professional considerations allow – with the assessed needs of the patient. This applies to matters ranging from the technique employed to the physical setting in which therapy takes place and from the number and identity of the persons treated in a given session, or series of sessions, to the length and frequency of those sessions. At the same time, the vitalistic therapist fully recognizes that there are no surefire "gimmicks" in therapy and that the presumption that there are, or may be – a presumption which seems to be becoming more widespread – is irreconcilable with his basic concept of, and attitude toward, the patient, as defined above (paragraph 7).

The vitalistic therapist's flexibility with respect to the technique employed is implemented by a readiness to shift from one technical approach to another in accordance with the demands of the therapeutic situation. Thus, in addition to drug therapy and other medical techniques,[10] he may make use of such varied psychological methods as desensitization, role playing, confrontation, fantasy production, dream analysis, hypnosis, counseling, etc., and in either an individual or multi-personal relationship. But he avoids the tempting and vain delusion that any such method constitutes "the royal road" to therapeutic success and he is deeply mindful of the fact that any sense on the part of the patient that he is being manipulated or maneuvered may activate in some degree a negative response which is counter-therapeutic.

Since every therapist, regardless of his theoretical orientation, must have some goal in mind, however vaguely he may define it and however much he may deliberately limit himself to the expressed or implied goal of the patient, it follows that the therapeutic process necessarily involves the operation of values – "end" values and "instrumental" values. Inevitably certain things become "good" – namely, those which further this therapeutic goal – and certain other things become "bad" – namely, those which impede this therapeutic goal. The vitalistic therapist is fully cognizant of this fact and disclaims any pretention that the therapist can operate in a moral or ethical vacuum.

Indeed, for the vitalistic therapist an individual's basic attitude toward the world – in a popular sense, his "philosophy" – is a factor of critical therapeutic importance. He is concerned, however, not so much with the *specific content* of that philosophy as he is with the *quality of feeling* which underlies and surrounds it. He seeks to further the growth of a deep and pervasive *positive* feeling – of love, of dedicated purpose, of joyful enthusiasm – and to encourage the development of patterns of behavior which effectively translate that feeling into action.

In the light of what has been said in this brief outline, it is evident that the vitalistic therapist should be an individual possessing a broad range of personal and professional attributes. Among other qualities, he should have a deep rooted respect and compassion for all living things, a genuine, if perhaps quiet, eagerness for life, a capacity for easy and deep rapport, extensive knowledge of his field and of relevant fields, the ability to use flexibly and sensitively a wide variety of therapeutic techniques and a kind of worldly, yet philosophic, wisdom. I find it regrettable that among psychotherapists in general only relatively few can lay claim to these qualities. Nor are our specialized training institutes (including, I must admit, the one which I happen to direct[11]) giving appropriate emphasis to the cultivation of such qualities.

But here I am touching upon considerations which are of a pragmatic rather than of a theoretical nature and which relate not specifically to vitalistic psychotherapy but to psychotherapy in general.

1. See various Sections in Parts I, II, IV and V.

2. With regard to the Freudian goal of "making the unconscious conscious," let me point out that this phrase may mean, among other things: (a) directing the patient's attention to response patterns (i.e., defenses, action patterns, drives, etc.) previously unnoted by him; or (b) directing the patient's attention to the possible or probable origins or consequences of certain response patterns; or (c) dispelling the psychological obstacles presumed to be blocking the patient's awareness of certain response patterns; or (d) dispelling the psychological obstacles presumed to be responsible for the patient's repressing or otherwise inhibiting certain response patterns. For the vitalistic therapist, these are at best instrumental objectives, not ends in themselves; and the latter are considered risky objectives, since they presuppose a degree of psychological omniscience to which no therapist can legitimately lay claim.

3. See the Section, "Needs, Drives and the BT," p. 44.

4. That there are significant differences among individuals, and that it is legitimate to refer to certain patterns of response as "psychopathological," is not being denied, of course. See the Section, "The Genesis of Psychopathology," pp. 160-165.

5. See the Section, "Animism, Psychopathology and Devitalization," pp. 133-139.

6. This factor has been stressed, of course, by a great number of writers ranging from the Existentialists to the "Culturalists" such as Karen Horney and Erich Fromm.

7. See the Sections, "Needs, Drives and the BT," pp. 42-44, "Psychical Entities," pp. 95-100, and the first few Sections of Part IV.

8. See the Section, "The Nature of Psychological Responses," pp. 103-104.

9. Stimulation indicators are not "within" the body in the same sense, of course, in which, say, the liver is within the body. It is rather that their immediate causes, their neurological correlates, are within the body. They themselves, however, are present (have position) in our own "private" space and time. See the Section, "Metaphysical Dualism," pp. 56-61.

10. Drug therapy and other medical techniques (at least in their present stage of development) can operate only in a *gross* way in relation to a *broad range* of possible responses, not in a *highly specific* way in relation to *certain particular* responses. This is not to imply that these techniques are necessarily either *more* useful or *less* useful than non-medical techniques.

11. The American Institute for Psychotherapy and Psychoanalysis, Inc.

PSYCHOTHERAPY: SOME TRANSPARENT MISCONCEPTIONS

I should like to mention some misconceptions in relation to psychotherapy[1] which are held, at least implicitly, not only by many members of the interested public but also, it would seem, by a number of professional psychotherapists themselves. If to state these misconceptions is at the same time to make their falsity apparent, it must be remembered that even a truism is not always recognized as such.

(1) One of the misconceptions I have in mind is that psychotherapy, that is, treatment by means of psychological procedures and techniques, if perhaps not a science itself, is at least substantially *based* on science, in other words, on clinically and/or experimentally established psychological principles. But by its very nature, of course, psychotherapy as a form of treatment can be "based" on such principles only to a limited degree. For every situation in which human beings psychologically interact necessarily involves a vast number of *new* and *unique* factors, or combinations of factors, many of them extremely difficult if not impossible to identify yet perhaps *in toto* crucial in importance, which *could* not have been subjected previously to controlled study and analysis.

(2) Another misconception, no less transparent, is that through a painstaking exploration and "analysis," on a so-called "depth level," of a patient's early experiences, those experiences can at least to some extent be altered. Frequently associated with this misconception is the notion that the psychotherapist, particularly the psychoanalyst, is a kind of "psychological surgeon" who is able in some way to

"operate" upon the patient's past and thereby remove, or at least repair, some of the damage which then was inflicted upon him. Perhaps Freud's remarks in regard to the absence of time relations in "the unconscious" have served, however unjustifiably, to give support to this misconception. The fact is, of course, that the therapist can influence only the patient's *present* "psyche," that he can counteract or otherwise modify, by providing the patient with a *present* experience, only the *present aftermath* of the past.

(3) A third transparent misconception which might be noted is that short term treatment by a therapist, regardless of the particular approach he may employ, cannot be as effective as long term treatment by that therapist. But what is being overlooked here, of course, is the patent fact that impact can be *lost* by the extension of therapy – as by the extension of a conversation or a play or a musical composition – as well as *gained.* (The prolongation of treatment is not always, it must be added, the result of the patient's or the therapist's misunderstanding. Too often other factors, particularly the monetary self-interest of the therapist, may unduly extend the period of treatment.)

(4) Another transparent misconception is that inducing an anger-inhibiting patient to "express" or "release" his anger (say, by screaming or by using four letter words or by punching a wall) is likely, in and of itself, to be therapeutically beneficial. It would seem to me to be quite evident, however, that unless the *sources* of the patient's anger are diminished, little or nothing of positive or permanent value is apt to be achieved in this way – indeed, that if an anger-inhibiting patient is encouraged to *abandon* his controls, his difficulties may well be *compounded.* The employment of this therapeutic procedure, which is quite widespread, evidently is based on the presumption that it is analogous to the physical procedure of "letting off steam." But this is a false analogy, of course, since in most instances

the amount of "psychological steam" which needs to be "let off" is being continually regenerated. (Somewhat comparable comments are applicable to the "expression" or "release" of other feelings or emotions.)

(5) Finally let me mention the implicit but fallacious assumption that in the *therapeutic* situation changes in the patient's attitudes, ideas, patterns of behavior, etc. can somehow be brought about without having to take into account the conditions which admittedly govern learning in *other* situations. The fact is, of course, that, wishful thinking notwithstanding, no therapist is able to influence a patient, or anyone else, *except* in accordance with principles of learning which, as principles, have *general* applicability. Unfortunately, or fortunately, the exaggerated claim that the therapeutic relationship has a "unique" character can in no way dissipate this fact.

1. Here as elsewhere in these pages the term "psychotherapy" is used very broadly and includes forms of psychological treatment ranging from psychoanalysis to non-directive counselling.

PSYCHOTHERAPY: SOME PRAGMATIC CONSIDERATIONS

(1) The manner in which psychotherapeutic services are currently organized in this country seems to me in many respects to be wasteful and inefficient, with the result that, generally speaking, the cost of such services is too high and the effectiveness of such services too low. I would suggest that a *partial* solution of the problem lies in the establishment, in all metropolitan areas, of "distributive" clinics in contrast to the conventionally organized (hospital or non-hospital) "non-distributive" clinic. For the validity of the concept of a "distributive" clinic has been amply demonstrated, I believe, by the experience of the Community Guidance Service, Inc., in New York City, a uniquely structured agency which apparently has now become the largest non-hospital out-patient mental health service in the United States.[1] Let me hasten to add that the setting up of a distributive clinic requires only a negligible capital outlay and once in operation can be entirely self-sustaining!

The defining feature of a distributive clinic – and of CGS – is that it operates largely through the private offices of its affiliated staff members rather than through extensive – and expensive – facilities of its own. In consequence, it is able (a) to reduce its overhead costs to a minimum and (b) virtually to eliminate the heavy loss of professional time which inevitably is involved in traveling to and from clinic premises; and for these and other reasons, including the availability of numerous therapists having less than a full complement of private patients, (c) to offer its services at unusually modest fees. A further advantage of the distributive clinic is that its structure permits every patient, regardless of the fee he pays, to have the convenience, the comfort and the psychological benefit of being treated in a private office. Finally, because of the relatively unrestricted number of professional persons who can participate in such a service, a distributive clinic is in position to assign each patient, once he has been interviewed and evaluated, with maximum regard to his individual needs, a factor which often is, of course, of critical therapeutic importance.

Founded on the premise that the professional person has an obligation to the financially underprivileged as well as to the affluent, the Community Guidance Service requires both its regular staff members and its supervisory personnel to contribute a specified number of hours a week on a volunteer basis. It is the fees, if any, received from these volunteer cases, together with the service charges collected from other cases, which enable the agency to be completely self-supporting.

(2) Whatever we were to accomplish, however, in the way of deploying the therapeutic resources in our metropolitan areas more wisely, the hard fact would remain that the number of persons who would require (or at least who would be able to benefit from) some form of psychotherapy would greatly exceed the number who could be treated by the (individual and group) methods now in vogue. It would seem quite evident, therefore, that psychotherapists (a) must direct themselves much more energetically, in cooperation with other personnel, to the problem of *prevention* and (b) must make much more extensive use of *the media of mass communication*. Beyond this, however, it needs to be conclusively recognized that *our psychological disorders are in considerable measure symptomatic of the devitalizing nature of our society and that unless we can succeed in drastically restructuring that society, and with it people's basic attitudes, basic motivations and basic values, psychotherapists will necessarily be engaged in a losing cause.*

REFLECTIONS

1. CGS, a private, non-profit agency founded by me in 1953, currently has a staff of over 300 professional persons and is providing approximately 125,000 hours of treatment a year.

PART SIX

OF THIS AND THAT

REALIZING OUR POTENTIAL

If the universe is, as I have argued, deterministic,[1] all change is an unfolding, a fulfillment, a making explicit of what is implicit. Thus there is a sense in which no matter *how* a human being develops — even if it is in a manner which falls far below "reasonable expectation" — that development constitutes, given the environmental influences operating upon him, a realization of his potential.

However in a stricter sense only the *universe* is able to realize its potential. For only the universe is able to fulfill itself unaffected by anything outside itself.

1. See the Section, "Determinism Versus Indeterminism," pp. 65-68.

EXPERIMENTATION IN A WORLD OF CHANGE

We live in a Heraclitean world which is in a state of constant change or flux, a world in which no situation, at least in its most minute sub-atomic detail, or in relation to its overall context, ever literally is repeated. How, then, can it be reasonable for us to engage in scientific experimentation? We do so, of course, by presuming, or by trying to show, that the differences between certain situations, so far as they may be present, are irrelevant.

But we can never demonstrate that this is so, for the demonstration would have to presuppose the very conclusion we are seeking to establish!

MORALITY AND ABSURDITY

It seems absurd that the soundness of the moral precepts to which we may seek to adhere in conducting our lives, precepts which may alone give us a sense of moral purpose and a sense of decency, can never be demonstrated by any factual evidence.[1] In the nature of the case, any such attempt would involve us in what has been called the naturalistic fallacy, that is, the unwarranted transition (unless we arbitrarily *define* what should be in terms of what is) from what *is* to what *should be.*

Fortunately, however, it is only in our more philosophical moments that any of us are apt to be greatly troubled by the absurdity![2]

1. Some philosophers have held that there are certain basic, perhaps a priori, "moral truths" which serve to legitimize or justify certain moral precepts. But the notion of a "moral truth" is in my judgment self-contradictory, since truth is by definition a function of (dependent on) what *exists,* not a function of what *should exist.*

2. I suspect that some unverbalized recognition of this absurdity has contributed to the current emphasis, particularly in literary and artistic circles, on the theme that *life* is absurd.

LOGICAL EGOCENTRISM

It is virtually a commonplace that any conclusion which we may reach ultimately rests upon (i.e., presupposes) premises whose truth we must take for granted (i.e., whose truth we cannot derive, without becoming involved in an infinite regress, from more basic premises). Yet not infrequently a great many of us seem completely to forget this. For we also appear to believe that somehow our *own* basic premises, in contrast to their alternatives, are demonstrably true!

THE USE OF WORDS

The use of verbal symbols, particularly in relatively abstract (e.g., philosophical) discourse, in the hope of conveying to others what it is that *we* have in mind is little less than an act of heroic faith. For, fortunately or unfortunately, words do not, and of course cannot, have the one-to-one ideational relationship we so often assume they do. Moreover, if, with the view to clarifying our meaning, we resort to "explanation," we can only, in a way, make matters worse. For though our use of additional verbal symbols may serve to dispel *one* ambiguity, it will inevitably introduce a number of *others*. We become entrapped, therefore, in an infinite regress, an infinite regress, however, whose presence, for "practical" reasons, we arbitrarily choose to ignore.

DIFFERENCES IN PHILOSOPHY

Much of philosophy is a matter of providing different terminological frameworks – for the same picture.

FROM INEQUALITY TO INEQUITY

Those who advocate some economic, political or sociological change on the ground that it will reduce or eliminate some inequality – for example, an inequality with respect to the right to vote or an inequality with respect to educational opportunity – generally take for granted, as do those who are persuaded by the argument, that the reduction or elimination of an *inequality* is equivalent to, or at least entails, the reduction or elimination of an *inequity*. If we examine this argument at all critically, however, we will recognize that it is logically invalid since it involves the aforementioned naturalistic fallacy,[1] that is, the unwarranted transition from a *factual* concept (the concept of inequality) to a *value* concept (the concept of inequity).

It is noteworthy that nevertheless reformers and revolutionaries alike have made extensive (overt or covert) use of this argument. Indeed we may say that *ironically it is this fallacious argument which throughout history has provided the major rationale for the improvement of the human condition!*

1. See the Section, "Morality and Absurdity," p. 183.

HOW MUCH EQUALITY?

Today in the United States, as in many other countries, there is a concern about certain forms of inequality which in the past were almost completely ignored. For currently the thrust is not merely toward the assurance of certain legal and political rights (which in various degrees have been obtained) but also, and perhaps mainly, toward the elimination of personal handicaps, for example, those associated with one's ethnic or economic or educational background. Equity (justice) requires, it is argued, that those who are the victims of such inequality be given compensatory advantages.

This argument has a distinct flavor of reasonableness about it (despite the fact that it is less than logically compelling)[1] and, for me at least, a strong emotional appeal. But where does it lead us? If compensatory advantages – say, in the form of special opportunities or special grants – should be given someone who is disadvantaged in virtue of the fact that he is a member of a minority (and generally discriminated against) race or in virtue of the fact that he comes from an economically or educationally deprived social class, should they not also be granted the person who is handicapped in *other* ways, say by his low intelligence or his low blood pressure or his short stature or his unattractive physiognomy or his foreign accent or his effeminate manner or his obnoxious personality, etc.? For these factors too may deny him the opportunity to compete on equal terms for life's rewards,[2] indeed, in many instances may prove to be even more *severely* delimiting.

It becomes clear, therefore, that if our thesis (viz., that those having personal handicaps should be given compensatory advantages) is to receive practical implementation, we must arbitrarily favor *some* of those who are personally handicapped over *others.* This may very well be highly desirable. But to the extent to which we must proceed on an *arbitrary* basis, we are also proceeding on a basis which, in a sense, is discriminatory and without any moral sanction.

1. See the preceding Section, "From Inequality to Inequity."

2. Of the traits or factors mentioned, some are genetically based (as race is), some are the products of one's life history (as economic or educational deprivation is); and some are intrinsically disadvantageous (as economic or educational deprivation is) and some are disadvantageous (as race is) solely because of society's negative attitude toward them.

AMERICAN DEMOCRACY

Though a society can be so organized that everyone (provided only he meets certain qualifications) will have an equal *vote,* a society *cannot* be so organized, of course, that every *voter* will have an equal *political influence.* For by reason of more favorable position or greater involvement or superior ability, some people inevitably will be politically more influential than others.

If it is unrealistic to expect that political influence in a democratic society be distributed *equally,* it is *not* unrealistic to expect that it be distributed *democratically,* that is, in a manner which serves to further rather than to hinder the realization of democratic goals. Unfortunately, in consequence of its morally indefensible but deeply imbedded power structure, rooted as it is in racism and in the "military-industrial complex," American democracy today is failing to meet this demand. This is contributing to an ever more insistent questioning of the validity of the democratic process.

This questioning is also a function of the modus operandi of American government. For ours is a society whose governmental machinery is failing ever more markedly to keep pace with the accelerating rate of internal and external change. What, of course, is called for in this respect is a thoroughgoing "streamlining" of our governmental apparatus, at all three levels of government and within all three branches. But since such a change will require that the exercise of power be concentrated more narrowly at the top, it will need to be counterbalanced by distributing the *control* over that power more widely at the bottom.

Because the influence of the media of mass communication

can be so far-reaching and so decisive, both in regard to public opinion and public action, it seems to me essential that the communications industry be restructured.[1] Such a reorganization should be directed toward assuring maximal freedom of expression in relation to competing ideas; but to expose the public to content which serves to inflame rather than to inform, or to degrade rather than to elevate, is a "freedom" which no democracy can long afford.

In a sense, however, the basic malaise of American democracy lies not in its structure but in its values. Too few of its people have a sense of purpose which effectively mobilizes their constructive potential. To be sure, there are economic and social status incentives which may motivate an individual, in relation to himself or his family or, occasionally, in relation to his vocational or ethnic or sociocultural group. But these goals are likely to be to a considerable degree unfulfilling, either because they activate only a small segment of the individual's personality or because they are negativistically competitive.

I happen to believe that the human being, though capable of great cruelty, is also capable of great idealism and that he needs to have nourishing ideals almost as desperately as he needs to have nourishing food. Man is after all both a social and a philosophical animal and unless he can feel a genuine sense of identification with, and dedication toward, something beyond, and in a sense nobler than, himself, he is apt to feel isolated, belittled and devitalized.

1. The absurdity of requiring candidates for political office to spend thousands, even millions, of dollars in order to convey their views to the electorate, thereby, in effect, limiting candidacy to those who either possess or have access to great wealth, seems to me to be one of the more flagrant evils. Back in 1936, when I happened to be an independent candidate for the U.S. Congress, a modest campaign fund constituted a gross handicap but not automatic defeat!

INTERNATIONAL INSANITY

The spiraling escalation of massively destructive weapons, atomic, chemical and biological, seems to me as likely as not to eventuate in Man's partial or total annihilation. For apart from the recognized *technical* difficulties impeding a resolution of the problem, there are, of course, numerous and formidable *psychological* obstacles,[1] obstacles ranging from an obsessional need to save the national face to a kind of chauvinistic paranoia.[2] Yet I am not without some residual hope that before the midnight hour the major powers will come to recognize – in the words of the psychotherapist, "emotionally as well as intellectually" – that their weapons of mass destruction, far from adding to their national security, are actually endangering it and that it is sheer madness to be concerned about relatively minute socio-political differences in regard to *how* one lives when it is a question of whether or not anyone on this planet will live at all.

The accelerating pollution of the Earth's atmosphere and of its land and water resources is thought in some quarters to pose an equal threat to Man's survival. However here neither the technical nor the psychological difficulties involved are as overwhelming.[3] Indeed there seems to be some reason to hope that this danger, by fostering an unprecedented degree of economic, political and scientific cooperation, will actually turn out to be an influence on the side of Man's salvation.

1. In regard to the relationship between our psychological defense mechanisms and our survival, see the Section, "The Defense Mechanisms," pp. 147-148. Also see the Section, "Man's Aggressiveness and Man's

Future," pp. 155-157.

2. The International Council on the Psychological Dangers to World Peace, of which I am the Director, has had a special interest in the analysis of such psychological mechanisms.

3. Reducing a nation's level of pollution may call for technological changes which will be disadvantageous to it in the world market but it will not increase its vulnerability to military attack. Thus the psychological obstacles to international cooperation in regard to pollution are much less formidable than those blocking international cooperation in regard to weapons of mass destruction.

PART SEVEN

AESTHETICS AND THE ARTS

CREATION, ANIMATION AND THE BT

I regard Man's need (tendency) to create, whether through one of the art forms or otherwise, not, in the manner of Freud, as "a sublimation of the sexual drive" but rather as *another manifestation of the BT*.[1] In creating, Man is fulfilling with particular effectiveness his need (tendency) to *vitalize* himself – and, significantly, creation characteristically is accompanied by a strong *feeling* of vitalization.

This feeling of vitalization derives not only *directly* from the creative experience itself but also *indirectly* from the product created. For in fashioning any object – or any idea – Man is to some extent projecting himself upon the world in which he lives. He is thus to some extent *animating* that world and by this means *animating himself*.[2] Where the product created is very *highly* animated – Freud might say highly "cathected" – it is perceived by the creator as virtually a part of himself.

Man's extension of himself in this way is also, therefore, a way of *perpetuating* or *memorializing* himself.

1. See the Section, "Needs, Drives and the BT," pp. 42-44.
2. See the Section, "Animism, Psychopathology and Devitalization," pp. 136-137.

FROM ATTRACTIVENESS TO BEAUTY

As prehistoric Man interacted with the world in which he was living, he must have found that certain sensory patterns (e.g., certain visual patterns or certain auditory patterns) were literally more "attractive" to him than certain others, that is, *were more successful in securing and maintaining his attention or interest.* Some of these patterns must have been perceptually more attractive partly, at least, in virtue of their association with certain of his life experiences, for example, his experiences in relation to hunting or eating or fighting, etc., others, solely in virtue of their own properties, that is, independently of those experiences. *I would suggest that, in either case, the elicitation by certain sensory patterns of this form of maximizing (positive) response was, in accordance with the BT, a result of their greater capacity to vitalize him and, further, that the notion that certain entities are "attractive" in a metaphorical sense or, as we may say, "beautiful" (or have some other positive aesthetic value), developed slowly out of the fact that certain sensory patterns were "attractive" in this literal sense.*

Of the kinds of sensory patterns to which we apply the term "beautiful" today, there are some whose vitalizing impact and literal attractiveness continue to be quite evident — for example, the sensory pattern which is present when we hear a particularly "attractive," or as we may say "beautiful," melody or when we find ourselves in the midst of a particularly "attractive," or as we may say "beautiful," landscape or when we see a particularly "attractive," or as we may say "beautiful," sex object.

However, as Man's responses have become more and more intellectualized and more and more sophisticated, so too have his aesthetic standards, with the result that the original criterion of vitalizing impact and literal attractiveness has to a considerable extent been set aside.[1] Small wonder, then, that contemporary works of art (whether in the area of fine art or "serious" music) reflect so few of the basic or primitive sensory patterns in which the idea of beauty is rooted. Small wonder, too, that those of us who can be candid about the matter find so little in contemporary art which is deeply and durably vitalizing.[2]

1. As aesthetic standards became more and more sophisticated, it became less and less acceptable to regard utilitarian, particularly consumable, objects as "beautiful." In recent decades, however, such objects seem to have acquired or reacquired a considerable degree of aesthetic respectability.

2. I suspect that many devotees of art (whether of fine art or of "serious" music) have been vitalized not so much by the work itself as by the notion that their appreciative response to it gives them status — in other words, by its snob appeal.

AESTHETIC VALUES VERSUS ETHICAL VALUES

I have suggested that the concept of beauty has developed historically out of the vitalizing effect which certain sensory patterns had upon the perceiver. Thus aesthetic values appear to be rooted in the needs of the individual. In contrast, ethical values seem to be rooted in the needs of the group. They reveal, not what may be vitalizing to the individual, but what may be survival-aiding to the society.

RELIGION AND ART

Works of creative art, visual or musical, are generally described by the professional critic in free-floating multisyllabic terms which endow them with a kind of incomprehensible mystique. This serves to promote among the more imaginative, or rather the more suggestible, the sense of being able to reach out through art to the transcendent and the ineffable. Thus for these art becomes, in effect, a religious surrogate.

SEEING WORKS OF ART: THE THEORY OF VISUAL COINCIDENCE

I have long had the feeling that there was something radically wrong about the experience known as looking at a work of art. My concern has been only quite secondarily with the fact that if we do our looking at a busy art gallery, we are apt to be subjected to a variety of distracting sounds and, on occasion, to some annoying pushes as well. I am thinking rather of the contaminated content of the visual experience itself, of the fact that *because of the shape and size of visual works of art, it is inevitable that what we see also include much that we are not supposed to see!*

Nobody, I suggest, would seriously consider trying to listen to a concert if at the same time a dozen trombone players were tuning up at the back of the hall. Yet in looking at a painting or at a piece of sculpture, one is expected to shut out completely all the other *visual* stimuli which are simultaneously bombarding one's optic nerve. The fact is, of course, that one can't, that what one sees, and hence what one reacts to, is not merely the work of art itself, but its visual surroundings as well.

Since the difficulty stems from the fact that the boundaries of the art object fail to conform with the boundaries of one's field of vision, the solution, at least in relation to painting, is both clear and simple. *We have merely to construct paintings which are of such a shape and size that (given a certain vantage point and also a certain focal point within the painting itself) their boundaries and those of the viewer's visual field will coincide.*

What this means specifically is that paintings must have

the shape of a somewhat irregular horizontal ellipse, a special form which is not unfamiliar to students of optics. It also means, at least if one's vantage point is not to be too close for visual comfort, that paintings should be considerably larger than they are, though as an inferior alternative to this the artist simply might designate, pictorially or verbally, how the visible area evenly surrounding the irregularly shaped painting is to be completed.

In relation to sculpture, the solution is essentially the same, although here there is a minor complication resulting from the fact that unlike a painting, a piece of sculpture, when viewed from certain angles, may be visually penetrable, i.e., have "holes." The sculptor could readily deal with this complication, however, either by "solidifying" the object or by specifying the proper background "filling" for those holes.[1]

From time to time I have had the fantasy of expanding these field-of-vision ideas into an aesthetic theory which would provide the framework for a far-reaching new movement in painting and sculpture. By making pontifical reference to certain scientifically established facts concerning the physiology and psychology of visual perception, and by combining these with certain elusive philosophical concepts (couched, of course, in an equally elusive vocabulary), one might well be able to initiate a virtual revolution in art. I would suggest as the name of the aesthetic theory, "The Theory of Visual Coincidence" and I would propose that the practitioners whose art productions conform with the theory be called "Coincidentalists." For the moment, however, I am compelled to leave to others the mundane task of fanning the flames of the revolution!

1. In this connection let me say that I believe the painter or sculptor should also be expected to make clear his wishes concerning *other* important variables, variables ranging from the lighting in which the art object is to be seen to the vantage point and duration of the viewing

experience. For the impact of an art object depends as much on *these* factors, I would argue, as the impact of a musical composition depends, say, on its key or even its tempo!

PERFORMERS IN ART

An aesthetic inconsistency which has been troubling me for some time is that our society gives great acclaim to the skillful performer of significant compositions in the world of music – say, to a Horowitz or an Oistrakh – yet is prepared to give virtually no acclaim to the person who may skillfully "perform" significant compositions in the world of painting or sculpture. But if the rendition of a great musical composition may be deserving of "bravos," why not the rendition of a great painting or of a great piece of sculpture? There seems to be the notion here that whereas a rendition of a musical composition can be an "interpretation," a rendition of a painting or of a piece of sculpture can be only a more or less accurate "copy."

But is this so? I would say it is *not,* that a rendition of a painting or of a piece of sculpture, no less than a rendition of a musical composition, *can* have – and I would emphasize the word "can" – all the characteristics of an "interpretation." Presumably a musical "interpretation" is a rendition which combines faithfulness to the original with some degree of individual self-expressiveness. But certainly this combination of qualities may also be present, and to an equal degree, in the re-creation of a painting or of a piece of sculpture.[1]

I suspect that the prejudice which I am questioning here has some of its roots in the fact that visual arts performers, in actual practice, generally have been, and generally have considered themselves to be, copyists rather than interpreters. Perhaps also contributing to the prejudice is the fact that the history of painting and sculpture includes some quite notorious artistic deceptions. But just as there is no necessity for a painter or a sculptor to be a copyist rather than an interpreter, so too, of course, is there no necessity for him to be a fraud. One may be as nobly motivated, surely, in rendering Rembrandt or Rubens as in rendering Beethoven or Brahms!

Perhaps it will be argued that the musical performer, in contrast to the visual art performer, renders a greater public service since it is only when a musical score is converted into auditory form that an audience is able to derive any aesthetic gratification from it. But the visual art performer too has the opportunity to multiply aesthetic satisfaction. Indeed, unlike the musical performer, he is able to produce an object which itself can be a continuing source of gratification for an indefinitely long period of time.

1. Whereas it is possible to have two slightly different renditions of a musical score neither of which actually *departs* from that score, this is *not* possible in regard to renditions of a painting or of a piece of sculpture. But we can hardly conclude from this fact that the former undertaking is in some way, therefore, more meritorious.

THE CONCERT HALL

It has for many years seemed to me incredible, yet at the same time highly revealing, that at any orchestral concert the vast majority of the members of the audience continually direct themselves to the antics of the conductor. I say "incredible" because I cannot imagine what the conductor's tortured grimaces, flailing arms and often humorously absurd body movements could possibly have to do with the patterns of sound we are supposed to be listening to – much less how they could encourage any kind of aesthetic or other significant experience. I say "highly revealing" because if listeners are undistracted by such gyrations, I suspect it is only because they are so peripherally involved with the music itself and find even the ups and downs of the conductor's coattails more deserving of their attention![1]

Yet I would not advise the listener to focus instead on those who, through their bulging cheeks or saw-like hand movements, are generating the sounds. For expecting to enjoy a concert while occupying oneself with the visible goings-on in the orchestra seems to me much like expecting to enjoy a scenic boat ride while watching the machinery in the engine room!

For my own part, I confess, I prefer to do most of my music listening at home, where I can stretch out in horizontal comfort, melt unobtrusively into the welcome familiarity of my surroundings and even, if I wish, fall asleep!

1. I might add, more vitalizing. As previously noted, attention giving is a means of maximizing vitalizing stimulation.

ARCHITECTURE AND IDENTIFICATION

The box-like masses of steel, concrete and glass which constitute much of contemporary architecture,[1] though generally admired as products of engineering technology, have been widely criticized as examples of aesthetic design. Thus it has frequently been said – and I would not wish to disagree – that because of their repetitive regularity and oversimplicity, they are markedly lacking in visual interest.

But what, fundamentally, are the psychological reasons for such a reaction? I would suggest that there are two facts which are particularly pertinent here. One of these is that in itself (i.e., apart from its relations to other lines) a straight line, since its direction always remains the same, is less interesting than a curved line. The other fact is that in itself (i.e., apart from its relations to other lines) a straight line, since it does not correspond to any lines characteristic of the human, or other living, form, is less likely to elicit an empathic or identifying response. That is to say, it is less likely to be perceived as echoing something of ourselves. In consequence, it is less likely to give us any feeling of meaningful contact or communication.

I have included the qualification, "apart from its relations to other lines," for of course it is quite *possible* to have straight lines which are so related to one another, or to other lines, as to be substantially free of the two deficiencies noted. Thus, for example, we may have straight lines, even parallel straight lines, which are so juxtaposed as to give a *curvilinear* impression or straight lines which subtend a multiplicity of *different* angles to one another.

The fact is, however, that in the rigidly rectilinear buildings of today no such relationships are present. The result is a form of architecture which is apt to impress us as being not only dull but dead.[2]

1. I am speaking here primarily of our contemporary office buildings and apartment houses.

2. See the Section, "Some Miscellaneous Vitalization Patterns," p. 141, item 6.

LAUGHTER

Much attention has been given over the years, primarily by philosophers and by psychologists, to the question: What is it about certain situations which induces us to respond to them with laughter, in other words, what are the generating causes of laughter? Though the literature reveals a plethora of would-be answers to this question, none of them appears to have succeeded in gaining undisputed, or even general, acceptance. Let me try to set forth here, quite briefly, my *own* view concerning the psychogenesis of laughter.

As I see it, *laughter characteristically occurs when and only when some (human or other) "object" to which we are attending is suddenly perceived by us in an extremely belittling or minimizing (i.e., down-grading) perspective so that we suddenly feel freed (at least for the moment) from the necessity of continuing to take it at all seriously, that is, of continuing to regard it with any degree of respect or concern. Laughter is a spontaneous means of overtly expressing this abrupt change in our perspective (set) and the resulting sense of expansive release.*[1] *In such a circumstance, the situation inducing the laughter – or at least the reorienting factor in that situation – is felt to be "comic."*

Thus if someone is suddenly perceived as clumsy (say, because he slips on a banana peel) or as absent-minded (say, because he forgets to put on his pants) or as excessively frightened or as unduly exasperated or as extremely gullible or as puppet-like or as "funny looking," or for some other reason is suddenly perceived in an extremely belittling or minimizing perspective,[2] we are apt to laugh at him. For we are apt suddenly to feel liberated (released) from the necessity of taking him at all seriously, of regarding him with any degree of respect or concern.[3] So, too, if some other type of "object" (institution, activity, occurrence, thing, place, etc.) is suddenly perceived in this way – for example, if marriage or political campaigning or Mother's Day or a contemporary painting or Texas is so perceived.[4]

It needs to be noted that the shift in perspective must occur *suddenly* so that there is a *sudden* feeling of liberation. Further, one must feel freed from the necessity of taking the (human or other) "object" *at all* seriously. Thus one will *not* feel completely freed from this necessity if one feels that anyone or anything connected with the situation, including oneself, has been belittled or minimized in a degree or manner which one finds unacceptable. This may be the case, for example, where an ethnic joke relates to one's own group and one happens to be ethnically sensitive or where someone slipping on a banana peel is immediately perceived to have injured himself.

Various other subjective factors may also serve to facilitate or interfere with the laughter response. These may range from one's knowledge of the language to one's prejudices and from one's level of intelligence to one's mood or frame of mind at the moment. Suppose, for example, that one happens to be feeling extremely light-hearted. Under such circumstances, laughter is likely to be quite *readily* provoked, perhaps so readily, in fact, that the provocative situation will resemble only slightly, or possibly not at all, the *characteristic* laughter-producing situation described above. On the other hand, if one is feeling quite heavy-hearted, one may be virtually *unable* to laugh. At such a time, life may seem far too solemn a business for one suddenly to feel freed from the necessity of taking the matter at all seriously.

On the view which I have here outlined, it is evident that laughter is by no means necessarily correlated, as it is for Freud and for a number of other writers, with the release of *hostility* or *aggression,* unless perchance we should use these terms so broadly as to make them virtually meaningless.

Indeed, it seems to me clear that where laughter is elicited by belittling or minimizing references to atomic annihilation or to rising prices or to air pollution or to the heavy air traffic or to crime-in-the-streets or to other matters we may "secretly" fear or worry about, it is often associated much more directly with the discharge of *feelings of anxiety.*

Let me add a few words about two other theories of laughter. (1) It seems to be the view of the so-called "man-in-the-street" that laughter is an expression of a sense of superiority. But of course this view, at least if it is stated in this very general way, tells us nothing about what *specifically* induces laughter, nothing about the *distinctive psychogenesis* of laughter; and in addition it is open to the obvious criticism that there are a great many situations – indeed, a preponderant number of situations – in which a sense of superiority is present but is unaccompanied by any tendency to respond with laughter. (2) A theory which has received much attention in academic circles is the Bergsonian view correlating laughter with the seeming transformation of something which is living or at least life-like into something which is robot-like or lifeless, as if there had been a sudden congealing or blocking of an underlying "élan vital." This theory, however, is open to at least two objections: that it is unduly limited in its applicability and that it is based upon, or at least is associated with, a metaphysical premise whose validity is at best extremely dubious.

1. Where the conditions making for laughter are present to a lesser degree, our response is more likely, of course, to be limited to a smile.

2. In other words, in some degree as *impotent.* See the following Section, "Comedy and Tragedy."

3. In perceiving someone or something as "cute," the role of belittlement or minimization (of the much larger or otherwise more prestigious entity with which we "unconsciously" make a comparison) is quite obvious. Perhaps here, however, the release tends to be relatively limited, so that we may be somewhat more likely merely to smile.

4. When laughter is associated with punning or some other "play on words," at least part of what is belittled or minimized is language itself. Some word (or phrase) suddenly loses the unique (i.e., the one-to-one) relationship it was *assumed* to have with a particular meaning. Thus it is as if a joke or prank were being played on the word (or phrase) itself. Let me cite the following example. Question: "Which batter never hit a ball?" Answer: "Aunt Jemima's pancake batter!"

COMEDY AND TRAGEDY

Both comedy and tragedy exhibit Man's *impotence* in relation to the world in which he lives. In comedy, his impotence is portrayed as *momentary* and *inconsequential;*[1] in tragedy, as *enduring* and *disastrous.*

1. See the preceding Section, "Laughter."

PART EIGHT

CREATIVE ANIMATION AND THE BEYOND

CREATIVE ANIMATION AND THE SEARCH FOR TRANSCENDENCE

I refer elsewhere to Man's search for transcendence.[1] Here I would like to say something about how I think we can gratify that yearning for transcendence without resorting in any way to the false or to the irrational or to the incomprehensible, whether in the name of Mysticism or Religion or Philosophy or Parapsychology or any other discipline or mode of experience.[2]

For me the world and everything that comprises it is, in a significant sense, as indeterminate as a Rorschach inkblot, as amorphous as a summer breeze. Thus by learning to allow that world to awaken within us our dormant capacity for what I would call "creative animation," I believe our longing for transcendence – and for beauty – can be richly fulfilled.

Almost all of us must have caught at least a glimpse of this other world – this personally created world – in our childhood, as we waved before it the magic wand of make-believe. For at least at moments then ours was a world which seemingly was spontaneously responsive to our every wish and whim, a completely animate, exuberant world bursting with the vitality which infused our own bodies. Tragically, the vast majority of us have somehow lost contact with that world in the process of growing up. Yet the possibility of renewing that contact, of recreating such a world, is doubtless still there.

Too few of us city dwellers look up, up at the sky and the floating clouds. Yet there are wonderful trips to be taken there and not necessarily alone! I remember how I have sat at the head of a cloud, with my feet dangling, and glided effortlessly and endlessly through the silent space. Or how, at other times, as my cloud was dangerously changing its shape, I have dashed about wildly from one end of it to another or had to jump from one cloud "island" to another. Sometimes, I recall, I have stretched out horizontally and immersed myself completely within the cloud, floating along ever so softly, surrounded and unseen; and whenever I wished, I would reach out into the liquid sky around me and drink deeply of its cooling blueness.

Sometimes I have traveled to the sky in our special balloon. There was an on-the-street telephone booth I knew which became our "balloon station" – and our balloon too. For it was this telephone booth which, whenever we wanted it to, lifted us into the sky and wafted us away to any place we wanted to go. Another starting point for our trips was the floor of a coffee shop where each morning before going to my philosophy class, I used to sit and observe the slow changes in a sun-made dog-shadow we called Misty. From Misty we'd slide up into the sky on a narrow, rounded sunbeam – much as firemen used to slide down second-story-to-first-story poles to hurry to their fire engines. I remember that it was always extra fun going around sharp curves, since then we'd have to hold on to each other especially tightly – in fact, whenever we'd approach a curve, I'd make sure we were traveling at full speed!

On a block I used to pass there were some trees. One of these trees became especially our own or perhaps we became especially a part of it. We left notes for each other there, at "Treeny," and carried on long conversations with her. She too, like the sky and the clouds and the sunbeams, like the balloon station and Misty, became part of our "family."

There were thousands of other "objects" in this family, this world, of ours and each of them was as alive for us as we ourselves. These "objects" ranged from seashells to kaleidoscopes, from a dent on a table to a tiny circular piece of yellow paper which floated down to the floor one day from out of nowhere. They included paper weights which we liked to hold in our hands because they felt so smooth and cool and just the right weight, and pictures in a calendar book where we went to lie in the grass or to walk along a path or to visit someone.

There was one picture which had a kind of special significance for us – a picture of an Alpine Village in which there was a church. For often we sort of prayed to, or with, or in, that church, for all we wanted for everyone in the whole world. It was "Churchy" to us and we'd kneel down together in front of it. We didn't feel in any way constrained or awed by Churchy. Nor did we resort to prayer in any usual sense. We just spoke to Churchy, quietly and informally, as one person might talk to another he knows and loves. . . . Somehow I felt closer to Churchy than to any other "God" I have been told about.

There are no boundaries to this world I am thinking of, nor to the things which are in or of it. It is a world of playing and a world of dreaming, a world of sounds but also of silences – and perhaps it is the silences which move us into it most deeply.

Let me return now to my initial thought. The world which I have been suggesting is a transcendent world but one which in no way requires us to take refuge in what is false or irrational or incomprehensible. What it does ask of us is the use of our capacity for (what I have termed) "creative animation" – that is to say, our capacity so to orient ourselves toward the "real" world in which we are living, that it is perceived as responsive rather than as indifferent, as personal rather than as impersonal and hence as animate rather than as inanimate. In creating such a world, there is no pathological loss of contact with reality, no self-deception. But there is a moving out from the conventional world in which Man too often confines himself to a far broader world in which he can find his "soul."

1. See the Section, "Man's Basic Longing," p. 225.

2. The yearning for the transcendental is manifested currently, among other ways, in the experimentation with hallucinogenic drugs. See, for example, Dr. Sidney Cohen's *The Beyond Within*: Atheneum, 1969.

TIME

The human brain — and I presume other brains too — is like a motion picture camera, linking and fusing one instantaneous picture of the world with the next, thereby creating continuity. What actually exists is as slender as a sliver of sunlight, an infinitesimal fraction of a second surrounded by a nothingness we call the past and the future. Yet out of this we construct a world which, we would maintain, has persisted for billions of years.

I SAT UPON THE SHORE AND HEARD

I sat upon the shore and heard
The endless pounding of the rocks
And then a silent sound absurd
Mankind would measure by its clocks.

At last the darkness came to me
And pointing to the distance said:
"Beneath that cloud, beyond the sea,
The foolish think the day lies dead."

CONTRADICTION AT AMSTERDAM

That is a man who passed
Walking the quay,
That is a man-made mast
Saying to me
Nothing that is will last
Eternally.

That is the moon that sings
Wooing a star,
That is the wind that brings
News from afar
There is no end to things,
To things that are.

SPHERES

There are no edges on a sphere,
No separate this or separate here,
No very far or very near,
For limitations disappear.
If what's in time is curving too,
There is no old, there is no new,
And what is false is also true,
And you are I and I am you.

MAN'S BASIC LONGING

Much has been written about a basic and insatiable longing in Man, a metaphysical searching for a vague "something" that is beyond both his knowledge and his grasp. Some have perceived it as a yearning for God or for the infinite, others as a yearning for immortality, still others as a yearning for a state of Nirvana. Some, more psychoanalytically minded, have spoken of an unconscious wish to return to the womb. Perhaps what is being sensed here, however vaguely, is the operation of the BT, or rather the fusion aspect of the BT [1] – an archetypal urge for contact with that which is eternally vitalizing.

1. See the final paragraph of the Section, "The Basic Forms of Response," p. 12.

BEYOND THE FINITE

There are three worlds which we have seen,
One smaller than the slightest trace,
One larger than the reach of space
And one the "real" world in-between.
It's here, they say, we live and die;
Yet somehow I am sure that I
And love have found a way through you
From this world to the other two.

TOUCHING

Of the various forms of sense perception, it seems to be in touching that we ourselves can most readily control the nature of what we sense. In seeing or in hearing or in other forms of sense perception, what we sense appears to be "already there" – already arranged for us – and our option in the matter seems to be limited entirely to the way in which we *allow* what is there to impinge itself upon us. In touching, however, we can have a feeling of *creating*, in large measure, whatever we sense, for just *which* touches will emerge is very appreciably within our own control. We can press firmly against the surface of some (animate or inanimate) object or touch it ever so softly; we can readily extend the area of contact or readily diminish it; we can move along its surface evenly or unevenly, slowly or rapidly, in a way which carefully conforms with its contour or which carelessly or deliberately opposes it; and we can serialize and patternize the spectrum of touches we create in whatever manner we may choose.

There is thus a "language" in touching which permits us to convey a wide range of different feelings. The infant seems cognizant of this language long before he is able to understand the language of words. And adults who are deeply moved usually have a compelling urge to express themselves through touch. Perhaps this is not unrelated to the fact that touching was probably the first way in which, in the long process of evolution, one organism communicated with another.

Touching is also the only "symmetrical" or "reciprocal" sense. If I am touching something, that something must be touching me. Thus one is not alone in touching; the "object" – perhaps itself a feeling organism – is always touching back and touching back immediately. There is a reassurance in this no other sense can give.

WHAT WORD?

What word
Would I leave behind
To those who will never know me?
Perhaps that happiness is touching –
Touching another living being so deeply
That in that moment
The world stands still,
Or disappears,
And we are naked.
Touching, too, for the sake of touching –
The life-giving freshness of an ocean spray,
The luscious softness of a suckled breast,
The drifting clouds and drifting breezes.
And touching most the melancholy mystery of it all
And all its beyondness
And all its unanswered silence.

IMPERCEPTIBLE PERCEPTIBLES

The other day I was lying on the grass beneath a tree looking up through leafy windows at the sky beyond – and across my body was clearly imprinted an intricate pattern of sunlight and shadow. It was there so vividly that I had a compelling need to touch it and to feel it touching me. And there was a sadness in me when I realized I never could.

THE FOG

I found myself talking a few minutes ago about the fog that had been surrounding me and how it had begun to lift. But "lift" didn't at all seem to be the right word and I then said that what actually was happening was that I was being left at the center of an ever-widening circle or semisphere... Then I began to imagine myself floating away on the edge of the receding fog, looking down at the ever-growing circular island spreading out beneath me. Perhaps, I suggested, that was something of what the God of Genesis had seen as the Earth was being created. . . .

HIS BROTHER'S KEEPER

I had been sitting for quite a while in a room of silence when I noticed on the floor a dead butterfly which must have been there, of course, all along. As the silence continued, it seemed as if I were sitting with it in lonely vigil during its final, sacred hours. I began to wonder why I, a stranger to this butterfly, had been chosen for this priestly role – until I thought I heard and saw and felt the words, "his brother's keeper."

BLINDERS

There appears to be a wonderful unconcern on the part of domesticated animals who graze uninterruptedly in the fields as to what, as we might colloquially put it, "life is all about." Completely unaware of where they belong in the scheme of things, they nevertheless go about their daily business as if nothing could matter less. It is as if they were protected against the bewildering uncertainty and confusion in the world by invisible blinders.

Man too seems to wear blinders, though blinders which are in some degree translucent. And as Man acquires more and more leisure to engage in philosophical questioning, his blinders are likely to become more and more – perhaps overwhelmingly – translucent.

PERSPECTIVES

There is a tiny dog I know named Samson who, for all his bravado, must surely feel his heart sink whenever he encounters a full-sized relative.

How wonderful it would be, I suddenly thought, if by comfortably attaching a periscope to his forehead, he could hereafter see the world from a higher perspective! And if all of us other Samsons, canine and non-canine, could too!

ROLLER COASTERS

At most amusement parks one may take a ride in open cars (variously called "roller coasters," "racer dips" or "shoot-the-shoots") which move at breakneck speed up and down and around the tracks. Sometimes when I talk on the telephone, I like to think of my words taking just this sort of ride, dashing through the wires, up and down and around, laughing as people do and being especially delighted because they never have to pay a fare!

MY THOUGHTS

Whenever I have the opportunity to escape from the pressuring activities of the day and to allow myself the luxury of silent reflection, I find myself surrounded at first by my very familiar thoughts. . . . It takes time in either world to wend one's way to where one really hopes to go. . . .

GROWING UP

When raindrops come and spoil his day
An adult wonders why,
For only children know that they
Are ladders to the sky.

MIRACLES

My body is my prison,
But my avenue of escape;
Separating myself from you, from any you,
Yet at the same time being my only way of
  reaching you;
Condemning me to oblivion,
Yet opening up to me the transcendent and
  the eternal;
An impediment to my knowing anything,
Yet the only way of knowing I have;
Different from me,
Yet the only me there is;
Acting in response to my will,
Yet directing me;
Relegated to the lowly status of an object,
Yet defying all efforts to be understood;
Assuring me there are no miracles,
But itself the miracle of miracles.

CHATTERINGS AND DISCUSSIONS

Chatterings and discussions of this and that –
Of Mrs. Brown, of the moral responsibility of the scientist,
Of food, of sex, of world problems,
Of the weather, of someone's vacation,
Of injustices and of hopes –
A medley of words,
Losing themselves in the air,
In time,
Without a trace,
Yet leaving behind
A battlefield
Of those who have perished
Where some had hoped
To survive
Through relatives
Or books
Or headstones,
Revolving in space,
Transformed,
Unrecognizable,
Part and parcel
Of all that is
And was
And will be.

SELECTED BIBLIOGRAPHY

ARDREY, Robert, *The Territorial Imperative* (Atheneum, 1966)
AYER, Alfred, *The Concept of a Person and Other Essays* (Macmillan, 1963)
BERGSON, Henri, *Laughter: An Essay on the Meaning of the Comic* (Holt, 1911)
BROAD, C. D., *Scientific Thought* (Cambridge U., 1923)
FRANK, Jerome, *Sanity and Survival* (Vintage, 1968)
FREUD, Sigmund, *Collected Papers* (Hogarth, 1924)
FROMM, Erich, *The Crisis of Psychoanalysis* (Holt, Rinehart, Winston, 1970)
GUSTAFSON, Donald, ed., *Essays in Philosophical Psychology* (Doubleday, 1964)
HARTOGS, Renatus, ed., *Violence: Causes and Solutions* (Dell, 1970)
HEBB, D. O., *The Organization of Behavior* (Wiley, 1949)
HINDE, R. A., *Animal Behavior* (McGraw Hill, 1966)
HORNEY, Karen, *The Neurotic Personality of our Time* (Norton, 1937)
LORENZ, Konrad, *Evolution and the Modification of Behavior* (U. of Chicago, 1965)
LOVEJOY, Arthur, *The Revolt Against Dualism* (Open Court, 1930)
McGILL, V. J., *The Idea of Happiness* (Praeger, 1967)
MOORE, G. E., *Principia Ethica* (Cambridge U., 1929)
NAGEL, Ernest, et al., *Observation and Theory in Science* (Johns Hopkins U., 1971)
RIBBLE, Margaretha, *The Rights of Infants* (Columbia U., 2nd ed., 1965)
RUITENBEEK, Hendrik, ed., *Varieties of Personality Theory* (Dutton, 1964)
RUSSELL, Bertrand, *Human Knowledge: Its Scope and Limits* (Allen & Unwin, 1948)
RYLE, Gilbert, *The Concept of Mind* (Oxford U., 1949)
SCHEINFELD, Amram, *Your Heredity and Environment* (Lippincott, 1965)
THALHEIMER, Alvin, *Existential Metaphysics* (Philosophical Library, 1960)
THALHEIMER, Ross, *A Critical Examination of the Doctrines of Bertrand Russell* (Wm. Wilkins, 1931)
YOUNG, Y. Z., *Doubt and Certainty in Science* (Clarendon, 1951)

INDEX

(Not including Part Eight)

A

B

C

D

E

N

O

P

R

S

U

V

W